DREAMS AREN'T FOR PEOPLE LIKE US

CLIFFORD LEROY LEE

i

ISBN 978-1-964165-68-4

Dedication

*To the Lee, Noble, Brown, and Nealy Families,
which are some of the inspirational families that inspire me.*

Author's Note

The author wrote this book to explore the complicated themes of identity, survival, and loyalty in places where surviving is more important than pursuing dreams. The author of this story looks at how family, society, and strength of character affect lives that don't always fit the typical definition of success. In this story, a young man grows up in the rough areas of Watts and Phoenix. His journey shows what it's like to look for meaning in a world full of violence and suffering, where love and loyalty are both comfort and burden.

This writing reflects what it's like to live in a world where hardships shape communities and shared struggles build bonds. The author wants to show how strong you must be to get through this world, where every day is complex, and the line between right and wrong is fuzzy. This story looks at the decisions people have to make to stay alive, protect the people they care about, and find out who they are amid difficult and sometimes cruel situations.

Ultimately, this book wants to make you think about who you are, what your family and surroundings leave behind, and how much it costs to stay alive in a world that can seem hostile to your dreams. The author of this story wants people to understand how brave it is to fight

for your place in a world that often seems to be against people who
dare to dream.

Contents

$\smile\!\!\!\infty$

Chapter One:
Raised By Streets

Tell me why dreams aren't for people like us growing up. My big brother was born first, probably ignorant about the role he would be playing in this world. Then came I, the second-born who was kicking and fighting already, impatient to come into this world, and even then, I felt like I had a destiny ahead of me. However, what could my destination be when I never even got a chance to meet my father? Mother said he died in a car crash when I was still in her womb. Even as an unborn, I knew I had to learn how to be a man from somewhere else. I was rebellious from birth. At first, it was just my big brother and me, at least for the next three years, until my little brother Peanut was born. Then time went on, and my mother had her first little girl, my little sister. Eventually, I had another little brother. I called my family the first five. Family was everything to me. I know I was right where I wanted to be with my brothers and sister.

Growing up in the ghetto was hard, and living at the bottom was no easier. But I knew I had to hit the street one day, and the love for my family would bring me back at the end of the night. At a young age, I only knew stepfathers. With our family growing, I realized my brothers, my sister, and I would come to love Daddy as our own father. When my siblings and I didn't have a father, he was there for us to the point where he taught my mother how to hustle. She, in turn, taught her kids how to hustle so we could learn to survive and never go hungry again. My stepfather had his faults. He said that when he had to. He helped my mother move into a house on Sheraton, which became the biggest weed spot in Arizona. Some were making more money than I had ever seen in my life, right along with my mother. My aunt often came by to visit us as she was close friends with my mother. No one knew where this was going, but we knew it couldn't be good. About a year into living in the house on Sheraton, we were raided by the police.

My father went to jail, and my mother went on the run, accompanied by her five kids, to Los Angeles, CA. As a young thumb-sucker, I knew once we pulled into that Greyhound Bus Station in Los Angeles downtown, we would be in for the ride for the rest of our lives. We did not know what she was going to do. My mother left us at the bus station and went in search of a place for us to stay.

She was on a search for another stepfather in the bar down the street from the bus station. With pride, she came back and got her five kids with no thoughts of abandoning us. She packed us up, and we all went to Nick's house. As mean as he was, he never put his hand on us.

We went about living our lives with him for many years. We were living off of Main Street in central with him, and it became my first stop. Living in hell slowly grew on us. Going to some elementary school called "Learning" or "Western," we started our learning process

2

at a young age. Knowing we would have to become men real fast, my brothers and I started our life in a gang-banging world. We met a side of a gang that we would come to hate for the rest of our lives. As this gang set out to bully us, we would learn to survive as time went by. We went to the same school, but as a result, we had to move off of Main Street in central, 2 43rd Ave and Hoover. At that place, we had run into bullies who had instilled in us the fear of knowing what Bouillion was.

But that didn't stop us from trying. We continued our hustling ways by taking groceries to the people's cars and pumping gas. Nothing could get in the way of us making money - not even our bullies, chasing us from one end to the other. My little brother was more terrified of them than any of us. As the bullying continued for years, we tried to live with it, but we couldn't handle it anymore.

One day while shopping with my mother, me and my brothers ran into our bullies. My mother watched and told us that if we ran from the bullies, we would have to face her. Knowing we would rather face bullies than face our mother, we knew we had to fight.

As my brother and the bully started fighting, my brother started getting the best of him. Somehow, one of the friends of the bully tried to jump in, so I had to get into the fight. My brother and I jumped over the main bully who had been bullying us throughout our lives and then started beating the living daylights out of him. We felt vindicated. Our bully would leave us alone for a couple of days and get right back to trying to bully us again, but from then on, we wouldn't run. In return, we would just beat him up, and this went on until we moved to the Watts Nickerson Garden project. 115th St., where we ran into the notorious blood gang known as the Bounty Hunter Bloodz, who quoted me and my brothers, and we became known as a part of the Five-Line Bounty Hunter Bloodz. In the gang, everyone came together like family, and we couldn't help but want to get in. I got involved so deeply that I never wanted to leave. Along with my family, I had an extended family – a family I could kill and die for.

A gang-bangers perspective taught me how to become a person on the streets. Well, I first took to the hustle in the Five-Line lot, where money came in abundance. The more I saw it, the more I wanted, so I picked up my first stack and never looked back. My brothers and sisters would join me for a while. They were too young to join in the game, yet they still tried to follow me around. I wouldn't let them go as far as the sandbox, knowing as the streets were. However, I ran in headfirst. I was headstrong, learning the ropes as I went. At first, I was kind of running around like a chicken with its head cut off. But soon, I learned the ropes fast enough to become one of the hustling forces who delivered his hustle with the best of them, all the while picking up a trade that would feed me for the rest of my life.

When the streets weren't always nice to me, I learned to put trust in my homeboys, who became like brothers to me. They never stood in my way. They guided me in the ways of the streets, teaching me how to protect myself against every foe. I needed that from them. I was their pupil. I learned how to deal with the school of hard knocks. They taught me how to be grimy against outsiders. I had learned to hate all outsiders. If you weren't from the hood, you didn't deserve to live. It gave me an attitude, driving me against anybody that I didn't know. My family and my homeboys were my family. To me, that was all that mattered. I knew from there that there was no looking back. I was headed somewhere, and I was only later going to find out where that somewhere was. As long as it was about blood, I was down for it.

As my mother had always been strict, we learned the hard way that she didn't care how she punished us. I don't mean it in a bad way. But, she would beat us in front of people like it was nothing. My mother had some bad kids, so I see why she whooped us. Often, my brothers and I would be on the receiving end of these punishments, but my sister hardly ever got a whooping. She did get a whooping occasionally. Mama ruled with an iron fist. She learned how to be a strong black woman from her mother, but I never got to meet my grandmother. I would have loved to, as I would have learned a lot from her, like my mother.

Despite everything, she somehow couldn't keep me out of the streets. I started to love everything about The Blood. No one could talk me against the blood. Blood was everything to me. With me being devoted to Blood from the start, I grew to hate crabs. I couldn't believe people would join sideway-walking gangs, so I started to shoot at sideway-walkers just to show crabs they bleed red. I was never one to show a crab love while building up my cash.

My family and I lived as a poor family. I mean, we had food to eat, but you could tell we weren't living well. Despite having limited resources, we were a proud family accepting all the efforts our mother put in for us. Being a mother surviving on welfare, she did whatever she could. Somehow, she made ends meet. Most of the time, it was extremely hard on her, yet she somehow made it work. She was extremely resilient and taught me to be the same. These attributes made her not only my mother but also a father figure in my life. Being a person who didn't have a father, I always valued these things, and I'll eternally be grateful to her. My mother tried to set me on the right path, but how could she stop me? However, she tried to stop me with all her might, and I loved her for trying. My mother always knew what was right for her kids.

Although I endured hardship on many levels, I just tried to be normal. In a world where dreams aren't for people like this, I took my slim chances, trying to make it in this world. I was all on my own. My homeboys were my only source of support. Our motto was: "Nobody moves, nobody gets hurt." At the same time, I was picking up other things from them, like how to rob people.

Somewhere along the line, I started applying the things I learned to make money and going to 112 Street School. After school hours, we would often break into the school just to see what we could get our hands on. Sometimes, we found stuff that we could sell, and sometimes, we would find food. I was willing to feed my family in any way I could. However, this was only the beginning. Later, my homeboys and I came up with our own little gang called the Five-line Snipes, which was a young band of boys known for getting into all kinds of trouble, like stealing and venturing out to the mall. It was one of our shoplifting places. The first time I stole from the mall, I was no more than eight or nine years old. Even then, I didn't care about anything –neither about getting caught by security or the police.

As I continued to get away, it became a regular thing to steal from the mall. Just by working on my hustling, I always knew I would get into the game. I knew I was going to become the hustler of the century. Despite everything, I was doing everything to keep myself from becoming a bad kid. I already knew I wasn't doing well by hustling, but it was taught to us children by our stepfather. I learned from him as I watched him make money. Living in a dope house didn't help my circumstances.

I saw everything that went down in hustling firsthand. From a young age, I knew I liked what I was seeing to the point where I fell in love with it. It wasn't the love you get from home; instead, it was the love you only get from the streets. As I enhanced my skills in the streets of the Nickerson Garden Projects, I learned I didn't want to be anywhere else. I was home.

When I spent some time in Phoenix, I came to fall in love with my grandmother on my stepfather's side. She was a great cook, so she taught cooking to everyone. She taught them to open up restaurants and buy houses. It was the start of her hustling work, and no one got in Grandma's way - not even Grandpa, who was a money-maker too. No one could tell me that they weren't my family, as I came to love them with all my heart. Wouldn't trade them for anything in the world, especially not for my father's family, which was the side of the family that I never knew. As far as I was concerned, David was my father.

Next, I lived in Los Angeles and had the time of my life. I knew life couldn't get better. To me, it couldn't get any better than this. As I went into YG from BG, I got worse, but I wasn't alone. I had my homeboys who were following in my footsteps. As I would hold guns for the OGs, who were hustling in the Five Line lot, it was a far cry from me playing human dartboard with my brothers and uncle, who at one point was teaching me how to be tough. He was always daring me to do stuff - stuff that was crazy, and I did it. I was always trying to prove to my uncle that I was brave. Usually, I ended up getting hurt. However, time goes on, and everybody grows. Now that I was beating people up, I was more respected by people that I called friends in the hood. They were people that I never understood - not, at least until I got older.

As I went along, I learned more. Growing up in the projects was like going to school. There was always something to do or somebody to see around the corner, branching out. We would ride down all the crabs like it was nothing, with no one showing remorse. How could it be any different from living every day? And still, I wanted to do it, but I wanted more for some reason. Shooting crabs brought me to the ultimate high. It was nothing compared to living in the projects, which had been a part of my life. My big brother was throwing darts up in the air on a school playground. It landed on the top of a little girl's head while my little brother burned down the neighbor's house. But I guess we called this living, and I didn't care.

Part 2

As life went on, things were getting harder. Two more of my little brothers came to live with us. With a house full, our living conditions got more terrible. My stepdad, who was often drunk, lived with us, and he was always driving me crazy. He just always wanted to abuse us, which obviously wasn't good for us. But we had to live with it. After all, how could we learn to fight him along with our troubles on the streets? Our stepdad was especially brutal toward me at times, calling me his primary torturer. He tried to abuse me the most, but I tried to fight against it. Mostly, it got me in trouble, but I was tough. I felt like I could handle anything. I had to learn the hard way, and I made my rebellion known.

Ultimately, it led to my family following in my footsteps. The more I tried to chase them off, the more they wanted to be around me. I couldn't let go of the fear that something might happen to them. Therefore, I tried to keep them at arm's length, but they had their own set of troubles.

Of course, my mom hadn't known things would be like this in my life. She didn't know that dreams aren't for people like us, and because of that, I had always known that I was on my own. Momma was the backbone of our family. With all the things she did, her strength brought me courage when I lacked it. Even when she became a drug addict just to seemingly fit in, I felt like she could do no wrong. No matter what she did, I still loved her wholeheartedly. I was unable to comprehend how she could deal with the likes of me. For us, living off the main and central was the worst.

As I had become a project kid, nothing and no one could get me out of these projects. I was also dealing with my fair share of bullies, but I learned to prevail through them. But life goes on, and everybody grows. I still remember when we got the news that we were moving to the Nickerson Garden Projects. It was like the world had opened up, and I had just begun to see things for what they truly were. I was so glad we moved because back there, in the main and central areas, there were no dreams. Boy, how did I hate the neighborhood we just left? Shifting to a new place, we had more rooms to play in, and more rooms meant more space. I just loved it. I couldn't believe I was finally home. Little did I know this would be the place where I would face madness. When we left our old neighborhood, there were not that many people to say goodbye to. We were set and ready to leave. There was nothing that could hold me back. All I could say was good riddance because there were no dreams there. Living in this new neighborhood, we were exposed to new surroundings. The first thing that we did was sign up for school the next day after leaving W. Vernon for 112 street school.

Chapter Two:
Crabs And Bloods

112 Street School was the place where I learned the wrath of being a poor kid in the projects. It was a place where I tried to fit in, but our poverty always made me feel like a fish out of the water. However, the fights I would get in made me tougher. In this school, I came across a bully named Derrick, who talked about my clothes for the better part of two years. It made me feel low until I couldn't take it anymore. So, we got into a fight, and I beat the crap out of him. Consequently, he never picked on me again. It made me revolt, and I became fierce with my fists. I fought my way through a lot of bullies.

I became a hero to most like me. My first two years went without a hitch. My third year at the school was my most memorable year. I loved my third-grade teacher, Miss Warren, like a mother, as she taught me a lot. But as my confidence grew, I became more and more of the person that I most hated. I myself had become a bully, but that's what got me through the rest of the years at school.

Back in the hood, I was making friends left and right - friends who influenced me in a way that made me realize what I could be. But who knew what it was? Later on, I learned that the Nickerson Garden projects were the biggest projects on the West Coast, stretching from 108 street between Compton and central all the way to Imperial Ave. However, living somewhere where society didn't care about our dreams was impossible. Things were different here. Our minds could go places, and I let my mind go anywhere my little legs could take it. Outside those projects was a whole new world with a lot of interesting things. I was still young and still in school, and my first crush was teaching me how to grow from a third-grader's point of view. I didn't realize for a while that she was the one who would open up the world to me. After meeting her, I ran back to the Five Line lot with more perspective and a greater outlook on life.

With the Nickerson Garden projects being the stomping grounds of a lot of boy hustlers, any outsider coming in from the outside wasn't safe. In the land of the Bloodz, it was all for one and one for all, where the hatred for blue and the crab gangs of America were the enemy. We would die if we could help it, as adapting to the violence had become an essential key to my survival. So, I was ready for whatever crab that got in my way.

When I met Perry in the hood, he became my best friend, and we ran the street together. As I roamed the projects, I made more friends, and everyone became a part of this homeboy thing. They were from the five-line, four-line, tray line, deuce line, and ace line. All you had to add was the boy hustlers to your group, and you had a full-fledge growing project of nothing but bloods expanding for blocks and blocks. No one knew what to expect from them, but they knew that the blood was to be shed in the end.

Learning that this was the biggest blood gang on any coast took me some time, but I grew to love it and grow with it. I felt like there was no need to stop there as I pressed forward outside of the project. In LA, there was always something to do. There, I met my first drug dealer before even knowing what a drug dealer was. Plus, with him driving the first Lowrider I ever saw, made me want to be just like him. I fell in love with the car and his lifestyle. However, while showing off, he wrecked his Lowrider into a car next to our house. As he threw it away, he pulled up a new one the next day. It was just as clean as the last one. He did this all while showing me that the game didn't stop. I took it to heart, and with it, I ran. Manpower became more of my inspiration, and the next day, I set out to become a dealer as well.

First, I had to learn where to get the sack. With so many places to look for, it was quite hard to find a fat sack. Starting out with nothing only made it harder for me to get my first sack. But it didn't deter me, as I had plenty of time to pick up a sack. So I just went back to trying to be a kid locked in a grown-up world.

As I started to hang out with Devon, Cleavon, Perry, Unk, and tank, we became so close to one another that we decided to form our own gang. It was a branch off of the Five Lines called the Five Line Snipes. We were a force to be reckoned with. This was where we set out to make a name for ourselves first by becoming thieves, then graduating to armed robbers. We started practicing how to be a stick-up kid, and before long, we got good at it. We went to Jacking Malls, all the while using the bus system to get to our Jacking spots. Our destination would be anywhere in California.

In the name of bloods, being young, we would wreak havoc. We would hit pigeon cages and rob people on que like it was nothing. We played war games with other factions in the hood, but we never really turned the hood against the hood. However, as we ventured out, parties would get more and more dangerous, yet we constantly did what we had to do. Money and greed turned friends into enemies. Nothing else could get us to go against the grain against one another. As we went from Five Line Snipes to Five Line Bounty Hunters, raising through the ranks became natural.

I remember the first time I saw a corpse lying there on the side of the road with a broken jaw from the car accident we were just involved in. My big brother had a large cut across his face. I was awakened by the ambulance driver attending to me, just to be whisked off to the hospital. The next thing I remember, I was given a bath by a beautiful nurse. That lot boy hustler manpower was becoming an important part of our lives. As far as we were concerned, the money and the sack were growing, so we ran with it. Manpower handed down the sack to us, and while he was considered a hero to us, to everybody else, he was known as a drug dealer. There were individuals who could go to the enemy territories and make money. The intertwining of these circumstances with my personal allowance created a situation where it felt as though money was flowing from multiple sources. Still, I engaged in occasional acts of theft, targeting purses and acquiring wallets and jewelry, all in pursuit of personal advancement. This was done under the pretext of benefiting the neighborhood, as the experienced individuals, referred to as the "oh geez," dedicated their time and effort to the community. Subsequently, the younger generations, known as the "bee gees" and "y gees," followed in their footsteps, continuing the legacy.

Growing up, besides my mother, my sister, and my brothers, I learned early that nobody cared for me, especially not on this earth. I learned that causing havoc was the quickest way to get my stripes. As the streets gave to me, I thought I was now giving it back by attacking the carver mark crab gang. So, that became something that I would look forward to. I thought I was past breaking into schools, but I still found myself breaking into schools. Quite often, it got me chased by the police. Once, I almost got caught as my homie and I crashed into each other and hit the ground. But the moment I fell, I quickly jumped to my feet and ran. I headed straight back for the hood. Once I was back in the hood, I felt safe; I felt like I had gotten away. Even though my homeboy was caught and cuffed, once I was in the hood, I felt like I was never there – like I hadn't been in danger at all. Though I felt bad for him, I had other things to worry about.

After one night in jail, the homeboy was out and ready to get into more mischief. But everybody grows. Soon, I came to bump heads with another homeboy who wanted to run the Five Line Snipes. The matter was decided; the one who could stay out of jail the longest would be the person who'd have the most active chance at leadership. So, the homeboy and I wanted to stay out of jail long enough to acquire that title, but neither one of us could stay out long enough. The moment we were released, everybody knew where we stood, and we were no further in leading the hood. All we were was Bee Gees and Y Gees, following in the footsteps of the Oh Geez.

I was not one to be a follower. I knew what position I held and what part I played to the extent that all I wanted was to learn to grow despite all the pain. For a while, I endured all the anger aimed at me, and it hurt for a while, with my stepdad putting me down every now and then. I could do nothing but wish I was an adult so I could move out. My mother wasn't letting me move out, and one stepfather prepared me for the next. I only got more stepfathers as I grew up.

After being back at school, I and my friends were having problems with learning. We were being warned that we would be held back. Half of us were too old for our grade, which allowed us to pass to the next grade without being held back. Mostly, missing school was no help to us, and somehow, we learned what we could do. However, we could, and whenever we lived in those conditions.

I had to make up my mind. With carnage everywhere, I knew I had to grow up fast, as nothing in this world would let me stay a kid. Because of that, I never played again, and every aspect of my personality seemed manly. So, I knew I wouldn't let this kid stand in my way.

Ranked high amongst the leaders, the hood wasn't my only official ruler, as higher-ups in the hood were already there before me. I looked for inspiration from Bee Dog, the original Five Line bounty hunter, and blood homeboy Boobie who demonstrated great leadership. Working under him, I would follow him anywhere. I could be led by him through any war. He was known for putting in work; Boobie was revered. He was the one who ran the Five Line Bounty Hunters.

Even though all roads didn't go through one man, one man would try to go through all roads no matter where they led. It's strange where some roads lead you, like the road that led us to the carver park shooting. Over there, Boobie's little brother, Deebone, got jumped by some crabs. As approximately 30 Bloods assembled and mounted their bikes, each carrying guns in their pockets, I, like a dutiful student, also joined their ranks and prepared to ride, ready for whatever might come. What we did next didn't shock me. Riding through Carver Park, we unloaded our guns as we passed back through to the neighborhood. Shooting up the neighborhood wasn't the first for me, and I knew it wouldn't be the last. Sometimes, it gave me comfort to seek revenge. It was all done in the name of the hood. While "good things" didn't necessarily equate to hood dreams, they revolved more around hood themes. One notable event was when Drake initiated it all by unexpectedly shooting three members of the opposing gang, the Crabs, before us Bloods had even realized what was unfolding. He went ahead and carried out the act, then returned to inform us of his deeds. Following this revelation, the situation escalated, and as I departed, one of the Crabs fell to the ground. Continuing forward, I joined the other Bloods, and we achieved similar outcomes. Eventually, we made a collective decision to turn back and make our way toward the neighborhood.

Throughout my growth, I realized that I wouldn't progress much further without following the path of a soldier. When it came down to it, Bloods were united, as internal conflicts only served to strengthen our cause, propelling us to higher positions within the ranks. We followed in the footsteps of those who came before us, advancing together. Nevertheless, life back home, within the hood, remained good. My friends and I were getting along like we were brothers. We were one big happy family. But like with family, brothers do fight. And after the homeboy hit my mother in the face out of disrespect, I lost all respect for him. Never again would he be allowed near me, around me, or in my area. I couldn't get the order to kill him; I just stayed away from him. After that, to me, he was dead. You know who you are, Buster. I wouldn't say your name to show you any kind of respect in this world. But life went on.

In the hood, things were good, and the hood was the hood. But still, we had to get paid, and I had to try to get more than everybody else. Being that I looked at myself as the poorest, I just wanted more. But as the Blood Gang became a way of life for me, even if it was blood in, blood out, I didn't want out anyway. Can't stop, won't stop.

However, as we got the Five-Line Snipes together, all we did was set out to do what we did. And that was to see where our minds could take us. The Nickerson Gardens brought out the good, the bad, and the worst in me. But it also brought out the best in me. Being the best shooter or jacker seemed like a good thing, but what mattered more was being something that I could live with. That's what I was learning. And what better teacher than the hood? Even though murder was easy, living with it was hard. I didn't think of myself as a killer but more as someone who was living. So yes, I pledge allegiance to the red rag of the Blood Gang, for which it stands in the United States of America, where the Nickerson Gardens reside. It was created to be one bounty hunter, Blood Hood, under God.

Beating up crabs turned into a game of its own, where catching one meant that his companions would quickly scatter, leaving him behind to get beaten. In this turn of events, he would often end up battered and bruised, his body covered in crimson blood. It seemed that cowards always ran in packs, as they would flee the scene without hesitation, leaving him to bear the consequences alone.

For instance, one particular day, we found ourselves beating up this crab. It seemed like this crab had his blood shed blood for the first time because the moment he caught the sight of it, he went crazy. He started screaming at the top of his lungs. It spooked the homeboys, and they decided to flee the scene.

As the crab gave chase, the homeboys looked like they needed some help, so I ran after the crab. In a twist of fate, the crab decided to take his craziness out on me. Little did he know, I was crazier. The more he acted out, the crazier I got, leading me to beat him down. It was the way of the land.

Leaving the mall, we finally made it back to the bus stop. We got on the bus and headed for the hood. After bragging about the display of my red ragging, I went home for the night, and I slept with peace of mind.

Around the same age, I started to drink, with my choice of beer being old English 800. I didn't start drinking because of peer pressure. I just saw everyone else drinking beer, so I decided to try it and liked it. I didn't drink to the point of becoming an alcoholic, even though the circumstances of life were really harsh, and I wanted to escape them. Nothing in life came easy to me. I guess it was a good thing that I didn't believe in luck.

However, that encounter with the crab proved to be lucky. That was the day I came to be known as the "hitman" – a title which would stick with me for the rest of my life. The name was given to me by the big OG homeboy. It was in appreciation of the actions I had taken against the crab. The boy didn't know what hit him when I shot him. Countless people witnessed it, but I got away clean. I never looked back, and Hitman was born.

Though still young, while at 112th Street School, there must have been a reason why a young girl named Dana hit me in the mouth and took off running, only for me to chase her down. I couldn't catch her, causing her to get away. But in the name of sweet revenge, I vowed to get her back for swelling my lips. As the days passed, I still couldn't get revenge on Dana because she just wouldn't show up for school. So I let it pass, thinking she had gotten one over on me. It was the first time I was hit by a girl, and she got away with it. Life went on, though. Remembering going from BG to YG only made my reputation as a hitman grow, as my status was always to rise to another level.

With every passing day, I was getting more frustrated with life. All I was working for was the OG status. I knew I would let nothing stand in my way to get there. I wanted to become a leader one day, but I was oblivious to the fact that achieving that would become one of the hardest journeys of my life. Along the way, I would have to take bullets and shoot many others.

As summer was creeping up on us, I knew I would get time off school. I didn't have to go to summer school. This meant that I would have extra time on my hands, leaving me susceptible to more trouble to get into.

And indeed, trouble found us as we spent our summer robbing malls and catching the bus back to the hood. We would often have to change buses. On Figueroa and Imperial, we often had to change buses. While changing buses, we would run into some crabs that were named after a vacuum cleaner.

On the other side, we had the Denver Lane Bloods gang, homeboys who often got into fights with the vacuum cleaner fools. But as soon as we, Bounty Hunter Bloodz homeboys, saw the Blood homeboys after jumping off the bus, we joined in the fight against the vacuum cleaners and gave them the business.

As the brawl was coming to an end, the crabs started to retreat. So I started chasing after them, only to realize that I was the only one running. I instantly knew it was a mistake because they started retaliating by throwing large rocks at me. One almost caught me in the head, and it would have either knocked me out or killed me. However, my instincts kicked in, and I ducked behind a road sign. Most likely, that last-moment jump saved my life. At once, I turned on my heel and started retreating. The homeboys were holding up a bus for me, so I quickly went inside and made my escape.

It was what it was. Little did I realize the dangerous nature of the games I was playing with my life. For example, one such game involved taking 22 bullets and placing them inside straws. We would then toss them into the air, allowing them to fall to the ground. Our objective was to avoid getting hit by the bullets as they discharged. Sometimes, we would even toss them from moving cars, aiming for crowds of innocent people. All of this was done under the pretense of fun.

As I engaged in this lifestyle, I never knew why gang-banging chose me. I just knew that it had chosen me because I didn't choose it. Until further down the line, when we achieved a sense of harmony, we were truly in sync. It was during this time that I started to learn that you let no man tear down what God has brought forth. I knew I deserved a better life. I just had to get rid of this voice in my head telling me otherwise.

It wasn't until my final year at 112th Street School that I realized it. I had acquired a name that was no better than my madness. I just knew there was more madness to come.

I graduated from bubblegum and raggedy clothes to khakis, T-shirts, and Chuck Taylors, upgrading my gang-banging attire. Mostly, I chose to dress in red, taking immense pride in my appearance. Alongside my red rag, I felt untouchable, feeling no need to fear anyone or anything.

Feeling no need to get into trouble at 112th Street School during my last year, I started excelling in my studies. I was acing my classes and getting straight A's. I remember sitting down to write my first essay, which I chose to be about Abraham Lincoln. To my surprise, I was told it was the best essay in the whole school, and I was even asked to read it to the school. As my reading had improved quite a lot, I sat down and read it to the entire school over the intercom. Although I didn't realize it at the time, I would say it was a proud moment in my life.

Around the time of graduation, everything went smoothly during our graduation ceremony. I was proud to graduate with honors. Interestingly, a few of my friends also graduated, not necessarily due to their academic achievements but rather because of their age and size. It seemed that being too big for middle school played a role. For some of them, this was their last year attending school together. Now, as I prepared to enter junior high, I had the entire summer to plan my next semester of school.

I often wondered where my journey would take me as I headed to junior high. In a sense, I had a desire to attend school, as times were tough at home. The uncertainty of not knowing where our next meal would come from sometimes led me to get into trouble. Stealing to eat became a predictable occurrence, and it often felt like every child had to fend for themselves. Despite the difficulties, we managed to get by as best as we could. Learning the value of a dollar became important when our allowance came in from the welfare check on the 1st and 15th of each month. Although it wasn't much to be happy about, we cherished our mother's love and her efforts to take care of us. Our main goal was to make her proud.

Chapter Three:
Crossing Enemy Lines

With summer in full swing, we realized we had other family members who stayed on the other side of the tracks and were from the other gang. One summer day, without my mother telling us where we were going, she took us into enemy territory to visit them. I couldn't do anything but ride along, wearing my all-red All-Stars, knowing these blue snot rag-loving people would tear me apart if they saw them. Even though I was young, I knew that wouldn't matter to a bunch of crabs. Neither Sam nor Russell would have been able to save me from their homeboys, just as I wouldn't have been able to save them from my homeboys if they were all in my neighborhood. Thankfully, the crowds were none the wiser to us Bloods in their neighborhood, and we left their hood without any problems arising.

Upon returning to our neighborhood, the five-line lot, I witnessed an attempted murder in the first degree for the first time during that summer. Although I participated, I was merely following the OG's lead. How was I to know that this crab would attempt to get gas at our neighborhood station? From the moment he was first confronted to the moment he took his first punch to the head, blood knew he was about to die. With each punch and stomp, he came closer to that fate, and no one felt sorry for him. It was just another beatdown of a crab gang member.

At that time, the police were converging on the gas station, and it became every man for himself as Bloods scattered in every direction, heading back to the projects and the safety of the neighborhood. We thought it was just a part of our summer games, but as summer came to an end, the new school year approached. I had to attend a new school of a higher grade caliber for my 7th grade year, Markham Junior High, which was an experience in itself. I had never seen so many of the enemy in one place before. With my brother already there for a whole year ahead of me, I still didn't know what to expect. As the year brought more experiences that would last a lifetime, I just went with it, which opened up a new era in gang-banging for me. Venturing into new territory was more exciting than I ever could have imagined, and it became more about Blood than ever.

But as I ventured further from the neighborhood, I found myself getting into more trouble. In one Blood neighborhood, I snatched a little boy off his bike and was chased hard by the police. When the bike got flat, I barely escaped by clearing through a narrow path. This was just the kind of stuff we did to get by.

My next misconduct changed my life in ways I never imagined; it was the robbery that sent me to jail for the first time. In jail, I found solace in people who understood our struggles. They knew that dreams weren't for people like us.

Setting off for the robbery, I knew it was wrong in the eyes of the law, but that didn't stop me and my friends from targeting two homely-looking school boys who had more than us. We wanted what they had and were willing to take it by any means necessary. With our numbers, we strong-arm robbed them without needing weapons, despite the danger in Los Angeles. The beating those boys took must have been humiliating, but we didn't care; it showed on our faces and in our actions.

After taking everything from them, we left them bruised and scarred for life, thinking we were getting away with something, not realizing we weren't getting away with anything. Because we robbed them so close to their home, they ran and told their parents, who promptly called the cops. The police quickly arrived on the scene, causing the Blood homeboys to scatter in all directions in a futile attempt to get away. I remember running and jumping into the bushes as the cops rolled by, arresting my homeboys. With my Blood companions captured all over the neighborhood, I stayed hidden in the bushes and just watched. After everyone was captured except me, I had a strange urge not to let my homeboys go to jail without me, so I came out of the bushes and ended up getting caught by the police as I tried to casually blend in while walking down the street. That didn't work, as I ended up in cuffs. After we were all rounded up, we were taken to the sheriff's station and booked in for processing. We were separated by age, and my same-age friend and I were placed in the same cell.

I didn't know what to expect because it was my first time. I just sat there in bewilderment, not truly scared but more amazed, as one by one, my friends were being released to their parents. By the time they got to Bubba and me, who were the last two in the jail cell together because our parents couldn't be reached, we found out we would be staying the night. Only later did we discover we were headed to LP, which stood for Last Padrinos. It was a juvenile jail with cells for age-appropriate juveniles who were criminals or accused of a crime.

The drive there was long and rigorous, and I still didn't know what to expect. Looking back, I was more curious than scared. I sat back and tried to figure out the directions to the place so I could have my mother come to get me, as I didn't know where I was and where she was. I only knew that she was probably at home, worried sick about me. It took a whole week before I found out my mother knew where I was, and it took three times as long to find out I wouldn't be leaving with her anytime soon.

I learned that I was not yet convicted and that I'd have to go through the court process first. We were charged with strong-arm robbery and aggravated assault, so I knew I was in big trouble. Being told I was the main instigator didn't help my case at all. Coming to find out that we robbed the son of cops made things even harder for me. Everything was pointing toward my guilt.

As Bubba and I had no grounds to stand on for innocence, we rode it out and waited for trial. In the meantime, I was sent to XY, and Bubba was sent to GH, where we Blooded at the top of our game, surrounded by crabs. Us Bloods held it down, and Bubba and I would see each other from time to time on the rec field and in the chow hall. We chopped it up as much as we could when we saw each other, and seeing other homeboys from the hood made for a better stay.

Though most crabs were scared of me, there were one or two who would try to test me, and we would fight, with me coming out as the winner. Beating them up wasn't enough; I had to humiliate them, and I mostly did it in front of other crabs to show my dominance as a Blood.

As I saw Bubba from time to time, I knew he was still in this place with me, which, in a way, made me happy because I still wasn't alone. We only got to talk to each other when we went to court, which happened in two-week increments, allowing us to talk often. Learning that our charges of strong-armed robbery and aggravated assault weren't going away anytime soon, we decided we would fight them no matter what. Not fully understanding what that meant, we prepared ourselves. Bubba was in GH putting it down, and I was in XY holding it down. We served our time with pride and in stride.

Finally, after a few months had passed, we were headed for our trial date, which was business as usual for the court. The victims took the stand, and every single one of them picked me out as the culprit. As the prosecutor pointed out the suspect, all fingers pointed in my direction. However, when it came to actually identifying me, the victims pointed to my partner and said he was me. One by one, they all claimed Bubba was me, to my surprise. Once the last victim identified him as me, my attorney asked for all charges against me to be dropped, which was quickly granted, and I was let go. Unfortunately, I couldn't say the same for Bubba, who was convicted and ordered to come back for sentencing.

While I went home without him saying a word against me, I knew I was the one who had put in all the work during the robbery and aggravated assault. Nonetheless, Bubba held his ground and just took the charges. It showed me he was a true homeboy, taking my charges as his own, which only made him stronger.

Once the charges were dropped, I was back on the streets and back to the hood again, all the while thinking about Bubba. As weeks went by and I lay around the house, Bubba finally went back to court, was sentenced, and released. However, his mother wouldn't let him out of the house, so I didn't get to see him for days. Finally, we hooked up in the five-line lot, where we talked about him being free. As the night went on, we found ourselves back to what we were doing before we went to jail, like it never even happened.

Back at school, as usual, I found myself in fights and getting into trouble, leading to suspensions. It became a cycle, repeating itself after each suspension. On one occasion, a member of the Grape Street gang tried to bully me. He walked behind me, hurling insults, but I paid no mind. However, things escalated when he slapped my food out of my hand while I was in line. Hungry and provoked, I reacted by rushing at him and beating him down despite his larger size. After that day, he never bothered me again. Though I stood up to the bully, I still ended up suspended for the incident.

Later, I found out that Beaver, a buddy from the Deuce Line Bounty Hunters, had also beaten him down. He told me all about it. It turns out that the bully couldn't pick on anyone else after that. Little did I know that Markham Junior High would soon be experiencing my presence. Despite my reluctance, I heeded my mother's advice, knowing she was the strongest person I knew. She understood what we needed, and her guidance was invaluable.

My experience at Markham would be unlike any other in terms of gang activity. Gang involvement was at its peak. There was no school worse than Markham Junior High School, so elaborate in reputation. It was a school so revered that even the weakest of hearts begged their parents to send them elsewhere. After hearing the war stories, most parents complied. But not me. I felt Markham was the right school for me because of its gangbanging theme, so I fit right in, especially with the Bloods and Crips looking to make a name for themselves. It felt like it was meant for me as if I belonged there, but only if I was involved in something. In my first year there, I set out to establish myself as a Blood. From fighting to learning, I've bled blood, and nobody could deny it.

In that first year, I befriended a Crip named Red from Hoover, who became my best friend at school. Outside of school, we couldn't be friends, but with blood on my mind and Crip on his, we just went along with it. Not having classes together didn't hinder our friendship; we just ran with it whenever we did have classes together. Despite getting suspended more often due to my fighting in the first year, I still loved going to Markham, even as I found myself sitting in the principal's office. Eventually, he would let me go home at the end of the day because he couldn't reach my mother. It was because we didn't have a phone. Despite those punishments, I still enjoyed going to school. It was a place where even those society deemed nobody felt like somebody.

However, on one occasion, the bully I fought and I had to sit in the principal's office together for the whole day because we fought at breakfast. His mother couldn't afford a phone either, which led to us exchanging heated words. It ended with a mutual agreement that it wasn't over.

As I reflected on how society contributed to raising this menace with no end in sight, I couldn't help but wonder about my own future. Would I make it through to tomorrow with only God knowing the answer? Despite playing the school game, I continued to be involved in gang activity. Dreams weren't something for people like us, but I couldn't bear to see mine not come true. So, I rebelled against the world, which only landed me in more trouble.

But making it through my first year of junior high school set me on a path for what I would do next. No one knew, like me, that I wanted to be part of the hood. As I successfully completed another year of schooling, I resolved to stay in, telling myself that if I couldn't handle junior high school, then no one could. When summer came, I felt a mix of emotions I couldn't quite describe. It was as if I was hurt because school was out, yet it also made me look forward to the upcoming year. I couldn't hide my eagerness to return to school as soon as possible despite still being involved in Blood activities. Throughout the summer, I evaded the police, thus avoiding jail time, but I still managed to get into mischief. I just wasn't rewarded with a trip to jail.

Though the summer dragged on slowly, all I wanted was to be back in school, gang-banging. I couldn't understand why, if school was providing what I needed for gang growth, I still felt drawn to the hood. Don't get me wrong, my heart was good in school, but the hood kept calling. No matter how far you took me, I just kept coming back. With no clear future, Nickerson Gardens was home. Now, thinking it was good that school was starting again in a month, I loosened up a bit. I started engaging in stealing, robbing, and beating up rivals like there was no tomorrow. Carrying over my track and field running skills from 112th, where speed was crucial, I naturally joined the track team at Markham Junior High, where I excelled.

As school started two weeks later, I learned my schedule for the semester. With PE being my second class, it naturally became my favorite. The coach trusted me enough to put me on every team for every sport, and I proved myself capable. This led me to join the soccer team, which was comprised of misfits. Initially, I thought we were destined to lose every game, but the Misfits proved me wrong. We won our first game, then our second, and went on a winning streak, with one or two close games along the way.

With me as the only gang banger on the team, I protected the misfits from bullies on the other teams. As long as I was around, no one would mess with my misfits, especially as long as we were winning. We ended up going undefeated for the semester. My friend Red from Hoover and I remained friends, still sharing homeroom and a few other classes together. Our bond meant something to us. But as one semester ended, another one would start.

During PE class the next semester, I devoted most of my time to track and field. Even though the gang life inside me wouldn't leave me still, not even my coach, who was training me to be even faster, could shake the gangbanger out of me. Around this time, I began learning about ditching and started doing it occasionally. I remember one time I got caught by a truant officer, who took me to some jail-like school where I had to sit during school hours until it was over.

One day, as a newcomer to the area, I got into a fight with a rival gang member because the school was located in their territory. With the city scattered with various gangs, it was uncertain which detention hall you'd end up in. However, this wasn't for me because school was where it was at. Back in Nickerson Gardens, the homeboys thought I should transition from Five Line Snipe to Five Line Bounty Hunter. With their encouragement, I made the switch, giving as good as I got during the beatdown despite being outnumbered. This became one of those proud moments for me. I was no longer just a BG. I now have YG status, with OG status looking promising in the future. For the first time in my life, the future was looking great. Or so I thought. You couldn't convince me otherwise. Being quartered in only boosted my status in gang-banging. It somehow made me feel more mature, ready to hunt with the best of them. I became involved in every move the hunters made, playing not just for fun but for keeps, especially within my Bounty Hunter family. As days went by, I lived in the moment, leading me to my next endeavor.

Chapter Four:
First Loves And Fights

One day, I went over to Devon's and Clevon's house, where they had a live-in babysitter who would do anything my homeboys said, which was a plus for me in my eyes. I didn't know this would be the day when I would lose my virginity. On this very day, somehow, Clevon got the babysitter to do whatever we wanted her to do, and she was okay with it. Being compliant with our demands kept a roof over her head, as she didn't want to be homeless.

"With this grown woman giving us, not yet teenagers, head, she got ready. My virginity wasn't taken at eleven, but it was more like me readily giving it away at that age. I was more than willing. I even went first with the head job, making me want her vagina more and more, so I stuck it in, with Clevon urging me on. It was a day I would never forget. After that, it went on many more times, and my confidence jumped. As the days passed, I learned more from her, and our interactions continued to shape my understanding.

Because of the confidence boost, I landed my first girlfriend, something I never thought would happen. But I ended up with Umeka, who was one of the most beautiful girls in the projects, a fact I couldn't believe at the time. And the fact that she was Wen's dog's niece made it even better, as visiting him became a way to see her. It was during these visits that I started developing strong feelings for her. At the same time, my friend Bubba began talking to her best friend, Mia. The four of us became inseparable, always together. But that was just the beginning. In our circle, finding Hitman meant finding Shorty, which was Umeka's nickname. Word quickly spread that we were a couple, and hearing our names together was music to my ears.

Before Umeka, I didn't think girls liked me. Since we didn't attend the same school, we often missed each other. However, after school, we made up for lost time by spending the whole day together. I didn't realize that a girl from the other side of the tracks liked me as I was focused on Umeka. Eventually, I noticed her growing fondness for me through her actions at school, and I started to like her, too. Despite sitting together in our shared classes, our relationship couldn't progress beyond school grounds, as I couldn't cross into her territory due to gang affiliations. Nevertheless, being able to spend time with her at school was enough for me. Umeka, being the niece of the OG Wen dog, was the epitome of a hood girl, and I hoped to earn his approval to date her. Although dreams aren't for people like us, I knew I had to pursue her. Being with one of the most beautiful girls from the projects would be a significant achievement for me, so I resolved to win her over.

Once we got together, you would always catch us together, with me always trying to impress Umeka at every turn. She was a girl I really liked, and I could only hope she felt the same way about me. For the most part, I believed she did because she put up with me. She was my first true girlfriend, and that made me happy. As I ran around the projects searching for hope, I realized it was hard to find in such a place. However, she became my source of hope, making me want to stop searching elsewhere for it. When I looked deep into her eyes, I felt like I found it there, which motivated me to do my best. She became my inspiration, fueling my desire to take on society. For now, it felt like my dreams were coming true, even though there was nothing I dreamed of more than being with her.

With no escape from the projects in sight, I pressed on with love. Even though we didn't attend the same school, I often wondered why since I wanted to be with her all the time. But everybody grows, and those who grow apart eventually go their own ways—however, not Umeka and me. We did nothing but grow together. Up to this point, I hadn't even touched her sexually, only kissing her and feeling her. That was the closest I had gotten, at least so far. With both of us having full households, finding the time and place to make love seemed impossible. But my desire for her only grew stronger every day. I could only hope that where there's a will, there's a way. However, I believed there would always be time for that as long as we were together.

Little did I know that the girl showing interest in me at school wanted to take things beyond the school walls. Despite her interest, I chose to keep our interactions limited to school, not inviting her into my neighborhood. However, it was evident that she desired more than what we had. However, I couldn't provide her with the deeper connection she sought because my heart belonged to Umeka. My feelings for Umeka were the only romantic aspirations I could comprehend at the time. Given the complexity of my life, I struggled to navigate relationships with even one girl, let alone two. Surprisingly, the situation somehow worked out because they never crossed paths.

But still, "Hood" meant crossing the tracks to the other side, where we played a game of bottling crabs. We'd load the back of a truck with bottles, no matter what kind, and throw them at crabs walking through their neighborhoods. When we encountered crabs who knew me from school, the attack was on without hesitation. We didn't care about how badly we hurt them; it never weighed on our minds. Then, it was back to the hood for a celebration of our actions, which coincided with the time alcohol entered my life. I remember taking my first drink and instantly liking it, drinking every time it was available but not becoming the alcoholic rushing out to buy it.

As time passed, I returned to school without much thought about the weekend. Then, a crab approached me, accusing me of putting him in the hospital, recalling the incident when we bottled him. It had been four days since the altercation, and he had just recovered from his injuries. I was unaware of his hospitalization until he swung at me, seeking revenge, which was futile as I ended up beating him up. However, this altercation resulted in my suspension, as the counselor wanted me to stay at school all day since he couldn't reach my mother. But that wasn't part of my plans, so I scaled the fence and headed back to the hood. There, I met up with the homeboys and made plans to hit the mall for a bit of stealing.

With summer fast approaching and school about to let out for the summer break, it was the year when most gang bangers transitioned from fist fighting to gunplay, causing gang activity to hit its all-time worst. As the future looked bleak, it must have been luck that I was too young to pick up a gun. However, gang bangers were still dropping like flies, with massacres occurring on the first day of summer. With no empathy for the other side, how could dreams be for people like us? All I could think about was the possibility of getting shot from here on out.

Dreaming dreams were like bullets for me, but I was happy I didn't get left behind in school and was moving on to the next grade. However, that year, I didn't perform well in school as my intentions were elsewhere, leading to no interest in my 7th-grade year. I wasn't sure if that would change or not. Anyway, this was the summer for turning vacant projects into hangout spots, where we would take our beer and weed, smoke, sit, talk all day, and sometimes sleep in the vacant project. Some of the homeboys would even bring girls there, but I didn't. In a sense, I was still a virgin, still scared to bring girls there. There was only one girl I could consider bringing there, but thinking she probably wouldn't come, being a lady and all, in my eyes, I never brought her. When it came to her, I was a pure and nervous virgin because she was my first girlfriend. But as far as being with a woman, I had been with one before. I wasn't a virgin in the literal sense. So, shouldn't I have known how to reel in a girlfriend? I guess not. But I set out to learn. And guess who taught me? None other than my girlfriend.

Sitting there in a vacant project, I often pondered how the atmosphere could shift from peaceful to chaotic in an instant. However, meeting up with my homeboys was always a constant. We'd head to the mall for some stealing, which became our summer routine. Yet, as summer progressed, it turned into one of the worst recorded in LA history. Fistfights and knife stabbings escalated to gunfire, leaving no one safe. With each shooting, the body count rose, making it the deadliest year on record, making this the year the drive-by was invented, shaping the future in uncertain ways. With gangbangers increasing, armed conflicts also increased. It was no longer a game; it was now a matter of survival. It became a matter of step up or shut up. I finally picked up my first gun, not with the intention of harming anyone, but to have fun and show my skill. I aimed at a streetlight, hitting it with just one bullet, plunging the area into darkness. This was what everyone wanted: to avoid detection by the cops. As the night progressed, my homeboys and I took turns shooting out streetlights as we roamed the neighborhood. Although everyone knew the gun belonged to the big OG, we couldn't risk it being confiscated by the cops. We vowed to shoot them if they came, but we were just young, dumb kids. What do we know? So, after returning the gun to the big OG, we called it a night.

But then, wouldn't you know, a few days later, I found myself in a drive-by with my homeboys. Some cabbage patch crabs rolled up on us and started shooting. Luckily, their aim was off, so nobody got hit. Looking back, I was shocked to see one of the homeboys still standing there throwing up two BEE signs, as if he was caught off guard and couldn't run, and he didn't even get hit. I thought I was alive to see another day but with no hope in my eyes. I had to go home to a drunk Nick who only had one good quality - the people he knew. He introduced us to a family that adored mine, and I was grateful for that. But I hated Nick with a passion, as I could never forget his mean stepfather ways.

Even though Red and his family lived in a crab neighborhood, they came to pick us up from the projects every day to play at their house. While the adults drank, my brothers, sister, and I played with their kids in a big backyard with its own garden, eating both ready and not-yet-ready vegetables. But my favorite thing about this family was something else. They took us fishing with them. We would load up their van, which was pulling a small trailer for them to sleep in, while we kids slept in sleeping bags around the lake or pretty much wherever we wanted. We'd toss our lines in the water before the crack of dawn and fish for however long we wanted. I must have loved that because it's all I did.

Learning how to fish on my first try, I wasn't scared to hook the worm. I caught more fish than both families put together. Fishing stabilized me for a moment, and I didn't want to go back to the hood, but I couldn't shake the feeling that it was calling me. Even though I went fishing, every time they asked me if I wanted to go, I always found my way back to the hood. I was growing madder because the hood was growing madder. I like to think fishing was my outlet, but the stresses of the hood meant more. I learned quickly that you couldn't be a weaker family in the projects, or you'd get run over by the bad boys in the hood. Going through it, I now was a part of it, with me and my blood ones doing lesser families wrong.

When a liquor store caught on fire in the neighborhood, the unfortunate family got lucky, acquiring a bunch of liquor that seemed like it would help them out, with plans to sell it and all. And guess what my homeboys did? Nothing but take it from them, plunging their family into despair. What's particularly cold about it? These were close friends doing this to him and his family. But that's how the projects were— with you one minute and against you the next. This vicious cycle continued throughout the projects. Families didn't know if they were coming or going, and no one knew better than me how the projects would betray you. But everybody grows, which wasn't necessarily part of it. Smart ones came together, forming bonds against others and crips and whoever the enemies were. Knowing your enemies kept you alive, but it didn't come without the brutality of the streets. Like the homeboy family trying to protect their product, the streets were brutal. As we took their stuff, we wrapped that up, and the project reverted to the next best thing going, which was selling drugs. Cruelty wasn't intended, but it emerged anyway. "Share and share alike" wasn't the norm. Project folks just came out and took what they wanted, even if that meant taking from a friend's family.

In the projects, strength was essential to cope with numerous disappointments and shattered dreams. Dreams weren't for people like us; we had to fight to navigate the world with challenges constantly thrown our way. Survival skills were ingrained in us, even resembling a well-trained army. Holding onto what you had was crucial, as a bird in the hand was worth two in the bush. I often wondered if it was wrong to learn survival tactics when that was all we saw in the hood. Suspense, thrills, fun, hurt, pain, death, and murder were regular occurrences in my life, leaving little room for a semblance of normalcy. For me, this was daily life, a harsh reality where the streets could swallow you whole. The hood never waited for anyone; it demanded constant vigilance and adaptation. Here, the game didn't wait for a man or woman; it was a place where you had to learn how to keep up.

Now, at this young, impressionable age, I watched as gang bangers stepped up their game, causing the Nickerson Garden projects to be ready for anything. As the drug game picked up, the Nickerson Garden projects turned project kids into millionaires and big-time drug dealers. Everybody wanted to get into the game, as there wasn't a person you couldn't find without a sack. Even I would get chased out of the five-line lot by the big OGEEZ, where the money was coming in droves. As a kid growing up too fast, I still tried to get my sack off, but there was still time to play as a kid. We would often travel to Red's house, and when we came to think of it, Red's backyard looked like he must have kept every old car he ever owned.

One day, while playing tag in the backyard, jumping from car to car, trying to evade each other, we heard a loud thud and my brother went down in agony, screaming in pain from landing on his private parts. Somehow, he slipped and missed, landing on the edge of the car. Upon hearing the screams, I ran over, giving him a once-over.

Thinking nothing of it, we kids went back to play while my big brother went inside the house, still in agony, and lay down.

About an hour later, as we prepared to go home, still thinking nothing of my brother's accident, my mother instructed us to take a bath. My big brother got into the tub first, and we were in awe of what we saw next - his testicles had swelled up to the size of a softball. Recognizing that something was definitely wrong, my mother rushed him to the hospital. Unfortunately, Killer King didn't have the means to fix him, so they shipped him off to General Hospital, somewhere out in the valley, where they specialized in the surgery he needed to fix his testicles. After the surgery, my mother brought all of us to visit our big brother. I couldn't tell you how she found that hospital way out in the valley, but she found it.

Apparently, she had superpowers. When it came to my mother and her kids, she would do anything for us. For instance, she made sure his internal bleeding stopped, and although, he lost half of one of his testicles, my big brother healed up enough for us to take him home. He still had to take it easy. However, having one testicle wouldn't stop them from having sex with a girl because, by summer's end, he and Red's daughter started hooking up.

As for me, it was back to crab hunting season, so we went to the village on a mission, and wouldn't you know, two crabs ventured into the village town Hustlers' neighborhood. They were Bloods, but somehow, the crabs didn't care. With us there to meet them, we surrounded the two and asked them what they were doing over here. As I watched my Blood homeboy ask them where they were from, one of the crabs said, "We don't bang fuzz."

And then, when we told him to stop, he flat-out fuzzed us again. The homeboy caught him with a two-piece, knocking him to the ground as the other crab's homeboy stood and watched, with him saying "fuzz" again and again. We all rushed him then. I didn't know how to take him steadily, with him saying the word fuzz. He was ready to get beaten up, and he just wouldn't stop saying it. As he continued saying it more, we jumped on him more, never letting up until Park patrol came and rescued him. Then, and only then, did we run off, thinking we would never see those crabs again.

However, we ran into some females at the park who invited us to their house. My friend and I went there the next day. Little did we know we would be showing up to the crab's hangout. These females had nothing but crabs coming in and out of their house, which we thought nothing of until we saw the two crabs we had beaten up the day before. While at this house, no one said anything to my friend and me. Taking it in stride, we got the hell out of there, leaving one crab neighborhood just to head back to the Blood side.

Back in the hood now, where we were all five-line bounty hunters, and no one called us five-line snipes any longer because we had stepped into the world of big boys and played to play where the big boys play. However, venturing to the crab neighborhood to see the girls on different occasions started happening more and more often. We never got into the crab's territory ever again. On our latest visit to the girls' house in the crab neighborhood, we came by none other than the two crabs we had left for dead in the village park, and now they were out for revenge.

Luckily, the girls warned us that they had come by looking for us and would be back, giving us the chance to escape unharmed. We decided to avoid venturing to that crab neighborhood again and instead focused on catching other crabs in the park. During one of our outings, we encountered a known enemy from Grape Street, recognizable to us because he had a pass to our neighborhood as he was a family member of a well-known leader among the five-line Bounty Hunters. Although Blood wasn't present to protect his family member, who was at the park with other relatives, my blood companions and I took advantage of the situation and attacked them, beating them down. News of the attack reached the leader, who then officially revoked his family member's ghetto pass to our hood. Initially, we thought nothing would come of it, but upon their return to their hood, they made a phone call to ours. The big OG was furious and gave us a tongue-lashing, albeit acknowledging that the victim was from an enemy gang. Thus, there was no internal conflict among our hood's members.

Around this time, the OG homegirl and I had started getting into it, and she had beef with me, which led to us getting into a fight. She was bigger than me, built like a man, and I prepared myself to take a loss. Despite her size, she couldn't beat me. It was all her fault for trying to bully me, especially after I had just defeated my bully. This gave me confidence, even if she was a girl. From that day on, I walked like a man and refused to let her bully me anymore, much to her dislike. After all, she was a girl, and she couldn't understand why I wouldn't let her bully me. If only she hadn't been showing off for the other big OG homegirl, it would have never come to this. Word got around about what I had done to the OG homegirl, and my status grew a little more in the hood.

With all this going on, even bigger news hit the hood as one of the OG lot boy homeboys was sitting in his spot when the police chose that day to raid. Little did they know, he would refuse to go to jail, pulling out a gun and shooting the first two officers that came through the door, instantly killing them. This gave him time to get away, with officers in hot pursuit as he disappeared into the projects, to be free for another day, even if it wasn't for that long. Then came the hardships of the hood.

As we mourned the loss of a different lot boy to the other side, he met his fate while driving through their hood, mainly to pursue their girls. One day, driving through 118 Cheese Toast Crab hood, he was shot and killed by them as they lay in wait, ambushing him. After giving him a proper sendoff, revenge was in order. From this, I learned that the homeboys sought revenge without the crabs knowing who or what had hit them, resulting in no retaliation. However, that wasn't the end of it, as we sought revenge once again, only ceasing when we were satisfied.

Here in the projects, having a good teacher was worth $1,000,000 dollars. I often questioned whether a young boy was supposed to learn this madness of the world at such a young age, and the answer couldn't be no, because I learned it, and I knew the worst was yet to come as more and more crab shooting spread throughout the hood. Everybody was hearing about us Bloods putting in work, turning the Nickerson Garden projects into one of the most dangerous projects in the world. Tasting blood made us crave more, fueling our urge to seek it out. As that urge was being fed, it became fulfilling.

Moving forward, my hair started to play a factor in my life. Growing up, I would see kids with long hair, and I wanted mine to be long, too. So I let it grow, and long it grew. Interestingly, it seemed to make me more appealing to girls. I enjoyed it when they played with my hair, styling it into braids or ponytails. But I especially loved it when one particular girl played with my hair, mainly because I thought she was a female player who was involved with one of the OG Homeboys. However, she was secretly seeing my best friend, which I found out later. Despite this, I valued her friendship, particularly because she was also my girlfriend's best friend, and I could always count on her to help me out with my girl.

She would use me to find out about her man, both of them. Despite my reluctance to divulge much information that could get him or them in trouble, she would confide everything about my girl. I admired her loyalty, believing she was a good girl, but was I too young to care? I wasn't sure. Regardless, I was willing to find out, thinking I was somewhat of a boy ready to become a man through this path of love. With no righteous man in my life, I had to teach myself how to talk to girls, which I was very bad at due to my shyness. Sometimes, I would just sit there and stare at girls, not saying a word at all. Initially, I thought that was how you start a conversation with girls. Like everything else, I had to educate myself on girls, all while dealing with the challenges of the hood.

As fate would have it, a crab decided to throw a party for his birthday, inviting crabs from all over his neighborhood, who gladly attended. While they were partying up a storm, somehow, the homeboys got wind of the celebration for one of their crab counterparts. They went into strategic mode against the crabs, planning, plotting, and executing a drive-by shooting at the party. Their aim was to leave behind casualties, and they managed to do so before making it back to the hood. Word soon spread that the birthday boy was killed on his 18th birthday, along with a few more partygoers. The homeboys, considering it a successful day, went about their business as if nothing had ever happened.

Though hearing these stories made me somewhat enthralled with them, I would sit and soak them up, wondering if I would end up like my homeboys. After all, I was a product of my environment, and as I grew up, I began to emulate them. I let the hood show me how, not knowing where any of it would lead, which left me confused. But being a quick learner made me eager to absorb more. The more I learned, the more inspired I became. I never imagined not being around for it, as life kept me studying and growing. In a world where I learned that life is tough, this is my reality. This is where I live, and this is a Bloodz life. As the killings came and went, it all turned into a slaughter, with enemies and friends alike falling victim. Living like this, how could dreams be for people like us?

Seems like with all this revenge to right a wrong, how could I survive? While some of the homeboys made a living in the concrete jungle look easy, it was always hard on me. I had to live where two wrongs always seemed to make for a right. Confused by the notion of a body for a body to make things right, I started to open up. With that, I let the madness in—or did it creep in? Despite my girlfriend and friends keeping me humble, somehow, the pain still found its way in. Learning to live with this was forced upon me, and it sank in.

A group of us Bloods would venture out of the projects to find more excitement, like hanging out with girls in other Blood neighborhoods. Through these interactions, we learned about their enemies, and they learned about ours. Somehow, we seemed to coexist, with "blood in and blood out" becoming the motto of us Bloods. Nobody embraced that motto more than me. However, one day, while kicking it in other Blood hoods, witnessing the madness that goes on in your own hood, when Bloods killed a crab, it felt like the madness just continued for reasons unknown.

Other situations caught my eye, mostly hood-related stuff. In the Nickerson Garden projects, nothing shocked you these days. Word spread throughout the hood about a 9-year-old girl from the projects becoming impregnated—it was more likely to be expected, just another day in the land of milk and honey.

Finally, the summer was coming to an end, and it was time to get back to school. While everyone dreaded going back, I couldn't wait to get back to my ways of beating up crabs. Running into the majority of them at school, where anything goes, and where there was a will, there was a way. I decided not to get caught slipping, as slipping could get me killed, even if it was at school. However, I had been in and out of jail all throughout the summer for minor stuff, like stealing my mother's car and taking it for a joyride, before I even learned how to drive. However, that wasn't even my first driving experience. We obtained our first car through the car owner smoking PCP. He got so high and delusional that he jumped out of his car, stripped off his clothes, and ran down the street. Naturally, we searched his pockets, took his money and car keys, and drove off in his car. This is where I would learn to drive. My friend took the car to Belhaven. He told me to jump behind the wheel and go for it. I didn't hesitate. I just put my foot to the gas and mashed it. Taking off like a jet, I punched it straight down the street.

Once I succeeded in becoming a driver, another friend of mine who couldn't drive took over. Trying to mimic me, he hit the gas like I did. However, he lost control, wrecking the car into a brick wall and two other cars, flipping it on its side with me inside. Thankfully, no one was hurt, but I found myself flying out of the car and running down the street at top speed, heading straight back for the neighborhood. Since it was late, I went inside the house and went to sleep, only to wake up the next day to hear stories of how first-time drivers learned to drive at night. So I wanted to drive again. Stealing cars now become a part of my repertoire.

One day, while we were in the neighborhood, a family arrived in a nice car, so we decided to take it, assaulting the husband in the process. We grabbed his keys and drove off in his car. But as quickly as we took the car, the cops were called on us. They pulled us over in the car, leaving us frozen, thinking we were headed to jail for assault and grand theft auto. Then I decided to jump out of the car and run, prompting all my friends to do the same. As I ran home, a cop was on my heels who I couldn't shake off. He chased me all the way until I reached home.

Once there, I began running around my mother's car, screaming, "Mama, Mama, come outside." When the door opened, my Big Brother emerged and saw that I was being chased by a cop. He immediately told my mother to hurry outside. I continued running around the car until she arrived, only stopping when she forced me to halt. She gathered information from the cop about what had happened. I was handcuffed, arrested, and taken to jail. At the station, I learned that I was the only one caught, although my jail stay wouldn't last long because the homeboys convinced the victims not to testify by frightening them with stories of retaliation if I were locked up.

An hour or two later, I was out, only realizing that I hadn't learned my lesson. Released to my mother, I made it back in time for the start of the school year. However, school couldn't keep me off the streets, where staying up late still meant having to go to school early. If the teachers allowed it, you just ended up sleeping in class.

As I headed to school on the first day, I ended up getting suspended for fighting with a member of the Crab gang, who made me assert my presence. During my suspension, I would just go home and wait until it was over, then return to school as if nothing happened. Despite repeatedly getting suspended, I still loved going to school and tried to attend whenever I could.

However, situations escalated, and my friends and I went on a crime spree, stopping short of murder but causing significant harm to our victims. The police became involved, identifying us as suspects and initiating arrests. They apprehended me and about seven of my friends, all juvenile delinquent teenagers. The police were building cases against us, finding most of us at school, where they made the arrests, and the rest at home because they had ditched.

One day, during the second period, I was summoned to the office. Upon leaving the classroom, a cop grabbed me, handcuffed me, and escorted me to the office, ensuring I didn't get worried and run, though I had no intention to do so. Where could I run? I had no clue, anyway. My plan was to go straight to the office.

Upon arriving in the office, I saw one of my homeboys handcuffed and ready to be taken to jail, too. Sitting in a chair next to him, I asked him what all this was about, but he didn't know. It wasn't until we were taken to the station that we were formally charged and learned what was happening. Charging us took all day due to the multitude of charges against us. After spending the day in the cell, we were finally allowed to call our mother to come pick us up. My homeboy called and located his mother, explaining our situation, but I had no such luck. We didn't have a phone, and I couldn't locate my mother.

After that, I knew I wasn't going anywhere anytime soon. When my friend got the call to leave, all I could do was ask him, "Can you go to my house and tell my mother what jail I was in? And can you tell her where to come get me?" I think my homeboy didn't have any luck with my mother since after spending my entire day in the cell, nightfall had come, and I was handcuffed and placed into the back of a police car for my trip to Juvenile Los Padrinos Jail, also known as LP. This time, after leaving A and B, I wasn't placed in X and Y; I was sent to G and H since I was old enough to be with the bigger kids, although not quite yet old enough to be placed with the older kids.

As it was late, I just went into my room and went to sleep, only to wake up in the morning and see that I wasn't the only five lines bounty hunter there. Seeing my homeboy lifted my spirits. I was not happy to see him in jail, but glad I wasn't alone in this. However, that feeling only lasted about a week as my friend got into a fight with this Crab. He smashed him, and he was taken to the hole. Now I was putting this blood thing down with other bloods from other hoods. As a lone bounty hunter, I was now getting into fights with white boys who would sharpen their long fingernails like knives just to stick me. With this crab approaching me, trying to earn himself some stripes, he provoked us and we got into a fight. So, I smashed him out and went to the hole. After getting out of the hole, my time at the jail went smoothly. I did my time and got out a few months later.

After doing all this crazy stuff, getting into trouble with cops, and being in juvie a bunch of times, I finally realized something big. Even though I had some friends here and there and did some cool things with my homeboys, I kept ending up back in juvie. It's like I was stuck in this loop of doing bad things and getting busted for it. As I think back on all the stuff I did, it's starting to hit me hard. In the middle of all this mess, I always found myself realizing that dreams aren't for people like us.

Chapter Five:
Surviving The Schoolyard

Back at school, I found myself on probation, facing the possibility of getting sent to the youth authority. Even though I wasn't scared of it, I was determined to avoid it. So, I decided to focus on my studies, aiming to do well in school and stay out of trouble as much as possible. Surprisingly, diving into my books led me to unexpected adventures, opening up new excitement in my life. I hadn't realized how much I could accomplish through studying. And finally, I found myself having a different kind of fun.

However, in a place like Markham, where violence leads to more violence, conflicts often erupt. Some crabs took it upon themselves to beat up a member of another blood, sending him to the hospital. Even though he came back to school a few days later, he couldn't forget what happened. So, that very day, he went home, grabbed his dad's gun, and returned to the school. Without waiting for the end of the day, he confronted the guys who attacked him and shot two of them dead.

Then, he quickly ran away, jumping over the fence and heading home. As the police came to arrest him, he waited for what would happen next.

Finally, word reached me about what had happened, and I learned that all crabs at the school were on a path of vengeance. So, I decided to hit the fence and go home, not wanting to get caught slipping by some crabs. Running into my Big Brother, who was determined to continue going to class, I had to force him to hit the fence with me, fearing that he would be hurt. Convincing him, we hit the fence together and left. As all the bloods left, no one could find the bloods anywhere in the school. I knew this was temporary because I had to turn around and go back to school the next day. But I hoped, that hopefully by then things would calm down. However, the atmosphere at the school was such that everybody watched their back at all costs.

A few days passed by, but there was no added pressure at the school, even though the tension was still thick, too thick to be cut by a knife. One little spark could set the whole school off, but the day went smoothly, and school let out without a hitch. Three more days passed without any problems occurring. During that time, us Bloods learned that a crab leader had been shot in the head, putting the school on high alert again. Many crabs were hurting and seeking revenge. Upon hearing about the crab's death, the school tightened up its security, aiming to prevent retaliation and any further violence. Despite efforts, a few crabs got beaten up while attempting to seek revenge against us Bloods. The school became a war zone, and we found ourselves right in the middle of it.

Now, I was fighting twice as hard to stay out of trouble and do well in school. However, despite my efforts, I still ended up in jail, but this time, I was sent to Central Juvenile Hall. I didn't think much about the blood that killed the two crabs at school until I saw him there. He looked like he was facing the rest of his life in prison, and I could tell from the look in his eyes that he knew what he did was wrong. His eyes held a deep look of pain that was hard to witness as he stared off into space, wishing the pain would go away. I can't forget wondering how it must have felt and what went inside his head. He never made excuses for his actions and ended up sentenced to 25 years for first-degree murder, with a plea bargain as his only chance for release. Then, he was taken to the California Youth Authority (CYA), while I was sent to McLaren Juvenile Hall for boot camp to straighten me out.

During the 30-day boot camp program, I progressed to the next level of comfort within a week, where I had to complete calisthenics to advance further. Pushups, jumping jacks, and leg lifts were just some of the exercises. To move forward, I had to demonstrate my knowledge of boot camp rules, including no sirs, yes sirs, left turns, right turns, about faces, and more. Passing with a quarter bouncing off my bed, I reached a more comfortable level within the jail, and the hardest part was over. I could relax in my bed and watch as other kids attempted to make it to this side. With only two weeks to go, I observed the world without the luxury of a TV, as there were none in boot camp. Two weeks later, I was free, and the time had flown by because I found other ways to occupy myself.

Now free, I was determined to change my thinking, especially my mindset like that of a mad gang banger. Though it wasn't in my mind anymore, I still engaged in gang activities, just not to the extreme. I aimed to do well in school for better grades. Yet, things were tough at home, with my stepfather and I clashing worse than ever. He lacked inspiration in my life, and I aimed to rise above him, much to his dismay. Despite his attempts to assert dominance, he garnered no respect from us siblings.

Though striving for success at school was working for me, things were all bad at home. It was because I and my stepfather were going at it worse than ever. He remained uninspiring in my life, but I told myself I would rise above him. However, my stepfather was not willing to accept that, so he set out to make his presence felt. He forced it on me and my siblings that he was the man of the house. Him asserting this got him no respect from us, and his attempts to assert control over the household were met with resistance from us, especially since his words often fell on deaf ears. That's because when it came to stepdads, there was a lack of understanding among me and my siblings. It wasn't that we disliked them. We just felt they weren't meant for us. From what little money I made from my hustling, my earnings made me feel proud, and I believed I was the man of the house despite not contributing to bills. As my attitude began to wear on my stepdad, he pushed me even harder, especially compared to my siblings. Though Mama toughened me up, enabling me to hold my own. But with him being a full-blown drunk, it only worsened his situation.

Going out and coming home at all hours of the night made my stepdad feel like I had too much power. This, in turn, made him think I was undermining his authority, and this pissed stepdad off. But I didn't know how much it was eating at him until his anger built up to the point of no return.

One night, I found this out the hard way when he tried to make me stay in the house because it was getting late or it was already late.

I asked, "Who are you to tell me what to do?" As he was in my face, I told him, "You better raise up off me."

As I turned and headed for the door, he saw this as an act of defiance and a challenge to his manhood. Reaching for his machete, he came after me. Outside on the porch, he grabbed me and then placed me in a chokehold. He put the machete to my neck, saying he would kill me. He did all this in front of my mother and siblings, terrifying them to the point where they thought I was going to die.

Freaking out, they ran and got my homeboys. This incident was one of many signs that my homeboys loved me, and they showed it by coming to my rescue. Getting my stepdad to let go of me before the homeboys had gotten there, I ended up saying some things that agitated my stepdad even more. He got so angry that he took a swing at me with the machete, aiming to chop my head off. However, right before it struck me, my mother raised her arm up and blocked the machete, and in turn, she almost got her arm chopped off.

Just at that moment, the homeboys had arrived. Seeing this, they went crazy and rushed at my stepdad, trying to get him to drop the machete. After which, they instantly got on his helmet. With everybody trying to attack him, he tried to run inside the house. This is when the OG Five-line bounty hunter leader pushed everybody to the side and knocked my stepdad out with one punch. Seeing this, I rushed and repeatedly kicked him in the head, trying to inflict brain damage. Along with my homeboys, I put in work on stepdad, all the while waiting for the ambulance to come and get my mother. We didn't care if they took stepdad, as I think he deserved the consequences of his actions.

Despite all the drama going on at home, I still managed to go to school every day, where I was doing good in every way. With the next semester drawing near, I was given classes all over the school, from the Bloods' side to the Crabs' side. However, my last two classes were on the Crabs' side of the school, which was a problem. With my teachers wanting me to do well in school, I needed to pass all my classes, so I had to go to the Crabs' side. So, one day, a teacher sat me down and worked out a solution to the problem, telling me I could leave those classes 10 minutes before school finished, which allowed me to continue getting good grades.

This meant I would have a lesser chance of getting beaten up. However, there was this one time I got cornered in the gym by about 12 crabs, most of whom had felt my wrath and now wanted revenge. Unbeknownst to them, one of their own was my cousin. Upon seeing me, he told his friend, "You're not going to jump my cousin," standing up to protect me, which, if he wasn't family, wouldn't be heard of.

That day, I got a pass, for which I would return the favor, even though it was a challenge to go to my last-period class where crabs would ditch just to come after me. Thanks to the teacher letting me out early, they could never get to me. On my own, I made it through the year, which saved my grades and leveled me up to becoming an A-plus student. However, tough situations still occurred walking home from school, like when these two adult crabs pulled up on the blood side. They jumped out of a car and started punching this boy who didn't even gang bang, beating him up even though there weren't enough Bloodz around to help him. They abruptly stopped, jumped back in their car, and left. Dazed and confused, the non-gang banger didn't know what was going on as he continued on his way home. When word got back, they accused us of beating up on their little brothers. I thought to myself, he didn't even have anything to do with it. The way I see it, even the innocent get caught up in it. That's how it was in LA; it made no difference to most.

Finally, my mother came home from the hospital, still determined to stay with my stepdad with whom I still wasn't getting along. I could never forgive him for what he did to my mother, but I was determined to show him I was a man, whatever that meant in his eyes. He was determined that I wouldn't become a man, and while he physically abused us, we showed him he wasn't man enough to do that. However, he was skilled at mentally abusing us. Unable to tolerate it, I stayed away from home, only coming back to get enough sleep to go to school the next day. I never gave up on my schooling, eventually becoming one of the fastest kids at school as I was on the track team. I never realized how fast I was until I started overcoming everybody while running, showing that I was good at sports. Good at sports and academics, I felt like I was going places. Despite what went on at home, I was determined to make school work. At the time, it felt like my only escape from the dangers of greed at home and on the streets.

One day, things were tough in the neighborhood, and I was broke. My homeboys and I were brainstorming ways to make some money, so we considered panhandling at the chicken joint on the corner. However, the process was slow as many people kept turning us down. I was really desperate for some cash, so I carefully timed my approach, knowing it was all about timing. Then, as I watched a customer reach out with a $100 bill through the window, I seized the opportunity, grabbed it, and dashed away just in the nick of time. Back in the hood, my friends helped navigate the maze of streets to ensure our escape. We thought that $100 would stretch far, but after a few days, we found ourselves broke again. That's when we decided to snatch a purse, opting for a quick grab-and-go approach. We targeted cars stopped at red lights, scouting out which woman would be our mark. Once we made our pick, we swiftly broke the car window and grabbed the purse while they were waiting at the light. Then, using a small ball bearing, we busted her window and snatched her purse.

After that, we ran to my friend's house, whose parents weren't home at the time. There, we searched the purse thoroughly, hoping to find some cash. We hit the jackpot when we discovered three or $400 dollars. I had learned the grab-and-go technique from oh gees I had observed before, and as they passed down their knowledge to me, I got good at it. To this day, I've never seen anybody jump out and chase a purse down, mostly because of the fear of entering the projects. To truly understand the projects, you had to become a part of them, or you'd never truly grasp what it was like. There was no mystery to the projects; all you had to do was be poor to get in. Never believe it's a fairy tale; always believe what you hear.

The more we operated on the outskirts of the projects, the more the reputation of Nickerson Gardens grew as dangerous grounds. That caught the attention of the city of Los Angeles because what happened next shocked the entire Nickerson Garden project. The city, thinking they could curb crime around the hood, took it upon themselves to put up a 12-foot fence, which looked like jail bars and was green in color, with occasional openings around the hood. You had to know where to get in just to get out, but where there was a will, there was a way. So us Bloodz took it upon ourselves to make more openings, ripping holes in the gate every chance we got. Some only us Bloods knew of. Squeezing through one of these openings kept me from going to jail.

For instance, one day, this crab came to a Blood gas station, acting like he didn't know where he was. So we Bloods reminded him, intercepting him before he could leave. Once we surrounded him, the fight was on. Now, with the OG questioning him, I took it upon myself to take off on him, setting off the rest of the homeboys and beating him to a bloody pulp. He never had a chance. Then, going through his pockets, I robbed him, and along with the homeboys, we left him for dead, not knowing the gas station attendant had called the police.

As sheriffs crept up on us from out of nowhere, seeing the first car, we struck out, running in all directions. Just so happened that as I was running, I ran across the front of a sheriff's car, causing him to stop and jump out and chase me. Luckily, I ran through a narrow part of the fence, getting away, where he couldn't fit through because of his gun. One or two corners later, I had disappeared into the projects, running all the way to the Deuce line side of the projects, where I hid from the helicopter on the Deuce line homeboys' front porch.

Once all the chaos went down, I walked back to the five-line lot, learning no one was taken to jail by the cops, which made for a restful night in the projects. Sleeping the night away, we woke up to a fresh start, just to get into a gang fight with the Cabbage Patch Crab gang. Us Bloodz forced the issue, approaching them head-on, walking right up to the front of their hood, trying to entice them to meet us halfway for a rumble. But too scared to approach us, those Cabbage Patch Crabs just turned and ran as we showed them we were all about CPC killa. So we headed back for the hood. Well, once we crossed the intersection, the homeboy turned and looked back from the middle section of the lane to watch our backs. As he wasn't watching out, he turned back and was hit by a diesel. We learned the next day he would be alright, as he ended up with two broken arms. Bouncing back from a diesel hit, he felt invincible, thinking if a diesel couldn't take him out, nothing could.

As things got back to normal around the projects, which normally didn't last that long, we found ourselves getting into it with the Cabbage Patch Crabs again. They caught the "so light, so bright he was damn near white" homeboy slipping at the liquor store, where they walked up to him and hit him in the face with a gun, almost shattering every tooth in his mouth. Getting away, he ran all the way home, where the homeboys found out what had happened to him, prompting us to set it off against the crabs. He didn't know this had happened to him because we had beaten up some crabs from their hood a little earlier as they were caught at our liquor store. However, if you slip, you get caught, and catching them slipping and them catching us slipping happened on a daily basis, which made retaliation always be in order. Therefore, we went looking for the dude that did this to the homeboy, first gathering up to discuss how we would approach the situation and decided we would just go look for him. But with guns in hand, we couldn't find him, and for that matter, we didn't run into any crabs, which saved their lives that day.

Now, we returned to our daily routine of trying to make the projects thrive. Even though it was a place where refusing to swallow your pride could get you killed, it was frowned upon because the next man wouldn't swallow his. Everyone, including you and your girl, could get it, facing the retaliation. This reminds me of how two crab girls came into the hood and how wrong they were done after their affiliation with the crab hood was discovered, as they were shown no mercy. After being stripped of their clothes, they were groped and fondled. I could do nothing but watch in disgust as the oh geez encouraged the Bee Gees to do it. Then I watched the girls become live-in hostages as they were taken to an undisclosed location where I knew they would be raped. Having no part of that, I felt sorry for the girls.

Later, I realized they must have been allowed to leave. As they were let go, they hurriedly exited the hood, only to return with the police to identify their attackers. Walking through the hood, the cop car with the girls inside drove past me slowly, making me nervous as I thought they were going to point out anyone they saw. However, the cop car drove past me, and I let out a sigh of relief. But as they reached my two friends, who were brothers, it was a whole different story. The police jumped out and arrested both of them, revealing that they were the instigators who raped the girls. That's what they were arrested for, and the hood never saw them again.

Chapter Six:
Echoes From Nickerson Gardens

Back at home, the situation with my stepdad was getting more and more dire. He introduced my mother to two more of his friends, along with drugs. As my mother got hooked, things at home worsened. Sometimes, she wouldn't come home at all. Currently, she manages her responsibilities, like paying rent and stocking the fridge. But when she started using heroin and began shooting it, things took a darker turn. As kids in our own world, we didn't understand what was happening with our mother. We couldn't fathom anything stronger than marijuana. Reflecting on when PCP emerged, I thought that it was as wild as drugs could get. But with every new drug, the shock was just as intense.

Thinking nothing of it, we returned to our carefree lives and enjoyed them a little while longer. In the projects, even the smallest actions of the Bloods caught my attention, and I was drawn to the allure they possessed. The streets became my father figure, and here in

Parenthood Nickerson Gardens, I allowed myself to be shaped by them. It was like attending a Bounty Hunter School of Hard Knocks, where every experience became a lesson. I couldn't move forward without learning something from each challenge, whether it took a day, a week, a month, or even a year. Until I gleaned a lesson, I remained stuck, unable to progress.

Taking only what I needed to become wiser about myself, everything I encountered in the Nickerson Garden projects was a lesson. And I mean everything. It toughened me up on the outside, so naturally, I had to be strong on the inside too. It was here that I stepped into the drug game as if I were destined for it. My first sack came to me by chance, just lying there waiting for me to grab it. Without telling anyone, I headed to the five-line lot to see what opportunities awaited. That day, I made my first and only sale before being chased off by the OG, who accused me of encroaching on their territory and profits.

As this became more and more common, hustling became a challenge. But where there's a will, there's a way, and I had to find a discreet way to sell my drugs. The OGs often advised me to focus on school instead of the streets, but I made sure not to sell during school hours; it was strictly after school. Initially, it was tough to gain their trust, but I found ways to work around their restrictions and continue my business. Slowly, it became the norm for me. Despite not making much money, I still had expenses, so I resorted to stealing from the mall. Getting in was easy, but avoiding trouble on my way back proved more complicated.

One day, while being on crab patrol, I spotted two crabs getting on the bus, but they didn't see us. They didn't know the torture was about to begin. I was one of the first two to start swearing at them, and the rest of the homeboys fell in line, making it better for us and bad against them. But as leaning into these two crabs went fast, punches were flying everywhere. As it was a war on all crabs, these two crabs were no exception. Finally, making it to their hood, they asked if they could get off the bus. With the answer being no, they received more beatings. The crabs got worried we were going to take them back to their hood, and as the beatdown worsened, just then, the back door came open, which made the two crabs run for dear life, making it off the bus and back to their hood.

With none of us chasing them, we rode on the bus headed for home. Both us and the bus driver acted like nothing had happened. Since bus drivers wouldn't call the cops on us, we felt invincible. Little did we know that at the next light, the bus would sit idling because it was too early, even though this was the blood side of the light. The crabs we had just beaten up were on the other side of the light with their homeboys, whom they gathered to rush the bus. Jumping off the bus, I was ready for a gang war. I saw that we were outnumbered, but being in the Blood neighborhood, Bloods came from everywhere out of the works to help us, with both sides coming to the middle of the street for a face-off, where the pressure was mounting, with neither side budging. I caught this crab trying to creep in and rushed him.

Little did I know he had plans to grab this rock and throw it at my head, trying to knock me out, which would have put me in a world of pain. But there was this sign post that saved my life as I jumped behind it, and the rock crashed into it. So, I turned and headed back for the bus that was getting ready to take off. My homeboys were holding it for me, as they wouldn't let the bus leave without me. Getting on meant that was the end of the gang bang fight. Leaving Denver Lane blood gang hood, we headed back to our hood.

Enough of advancing on their advancing. As advancement meant heading back to the hood. But with all this going on around me, I found myself lost, unsure of what to think. Being stuck in the middle of it all, I pondered, is a boy born without a father supposed to go through this? With my father dying while I was in the womb, I wondered if I ever had a chance. I believed I deserved a chance despite what was left of my upbringing, leaving me with stepdads. Growing up with them was painful; they were the ones who taught me how not to care. As I started growing up, I carried a chip on my shoulder.

But I always made it back to the hood, where our war stories were being told to young gangsters eager to emulate us, hoping to become original gangsters themselves. The OGs never let their teachings get weighed down, and there was nothing like an OG being happy seeing his ideas and teachings passed down without a hitch. So, I set my goals on becoming the leader of the hood, based on the ideas of OGs, which was a big feat for someone so young. But just as that was happening, tragedy struck the hood. An OG went down; the OG lot boy hustler blood homeboy had been killed, shot by the family that owned the store across the street from the hood. This tragedy struck in an apparent robbery gone wrong, and the OG ended up dead.

Naturally, retaliation was in order. By nightfall, everyone had armed themselves. As the plan was set into motion, the OG lot boy homeboy jumped into a car and rammed it into the store, setting it on fire. Just then, all hell broke loose, with both sides starting to shoot, leaving the store and house riddled with thousands of bullet holes. Miraculously, no one was hit, and this chaos continued for a couple of days. As I watched things around the hood slowly return to their version of normalcy, if you can call any of this normal, I started to relax a bit. Or so I thought.

As the next day dawned, the cops gathered up all the homeboys they could name, trying to gather information about the shooting of the family. However, with no one willing to talk, everybody was let go. The hood was back, thriving again, where little sweeps like this would often clear out the area, and you wouldn't see anyone walking around. But just like that, it would be filled again. With no witnesses, there was no case. But all that was a thing of the past, and yet the future held more jail time for me.

I was arrested a week or two after the shooting of the family that left the OG for dead. It was during this time that I would, for the first time, encounter an Indian individual. Never having seen an Indian before, I didn't know what an Indian was. This person was drunk in his element, and he was instructed to urinate in a cup for a drug test. True to form, he urinated into the cup, still intoxicated from his experience. When told to set the cup down, he instead started drinking his own urine. I couldn't help but cringe at the sight, thinking he must have mistaken it for beer.

I did not know if I would be staying or not because I was in there for something small, but I was still taken from intake to one of the cottages. I was placed in lockdown because there was no room to house me. At first, I thought I was being punished by being placed in lockdown. As soon as I laid my eyes on my cot, I instantly lay down and went to sleep. After all, being stuck in uncertainty was driving me crazy. But I lived it down, finally coming out of lockdown after three weeks. I was then placed in the general population.

Fighting my way through, my reputation grew in the hood, as homeboys coming and going told my war stories, which reached all the way back to the hood. As I got out to a hero's welcome, my war stories lived on, with nothing but props rolling in. Coming home from jail was always a plus, and all this love made me want to prosper. Was I to prosper? Having strong family ties, I always thought, why was the world out to get me?

With school still being my number one priority, I went back. Only this time, my mother cared more than I did. While the hood was breeding criminals, I was at school, trying to learn how to get out of the ghetto. Being born without a father showed I didn't have a chance. But through my schooling, I was proving everybody wrong. I was thriving, and my problems just seemed to go away. I wasn't being harassed by gang bangers. I wasn't being harassed by the problems at home with my stepdad. I wondered: Could school just take all my problems away? Although my mother made up for all the lost love elsewhere, I loved her like she was my father. As my grades impressed her, I tried to get good grades to keep her impressed, wondering if it was wrong to start from the streets, studying and learning just to be better. The streets taught me a lot, too. I found myself hating those who told me I couldn't, blaming society. Why is it that I, a product of society, have been led down some evil roads? I tried to navigate those roads lightly, but still ended up carrying the biggest burden. Society only taught me to avoid feeling, so I set out to bury my feelings. In turn, I became a madman who only had school to calm him down. Who would have thought society could turn me so cruel?

After being cruel to me, upon returning to society, I reverted back to my villainous ways. For instance, when I saw an old lady carrying a big purse, so big that I just knew it had money in it, we snatched her purse in broad daylight. However, the lady, unsure whether to scream or not, put up a fight for her purse. My friend then pulled out his gun and attempted to take it forcibly, but she still resisted. As it was taking us longer to get her purse, we risked getting caught. So, my friend panicked and shot the old lady. Only then did she release her purse.

Panicked, I still ran with the purse. Though shocked at what he did, I was scared. For a moment, I watched him freeze up because he didn't run after me, causing me to turn around and pull on him to get him to run. Finally, back in the car, we drove off.

Heading back for the hood, just then, my friend who shot the old lady started acting nervous and stressed that he wanted to get out of the car. But with everybody calming him down, we managed to keep him in the car and made it back to the hood. There, we got out of a wiped-down car and set it on fire. Back in the hood, we were nervous but happy.

By the time the police found the car, everybody had calmed down to the point where we wouldn't be caught. All in all, that still didn't stop us from searching her purse, where we found a little money along with some other things that we could sell. After emptying her purse, it still felt heavy, but it was empty, so we thought nothing of it and put it up for safekeeping, as something kept telling me not to throw the purse away.

Weeks went by, and still, I hadn't seen the homeboy who shot the old lady. So I went to his house, where he was barricaded in his room and scared to come out. He told me how he couldn't sleep from the nightmares he was getting from the shooting and that he would peek out the window at every car, thinking it was the police coming to get him. With my friend stressing beyond repair, it seemed like no one could help. After staying in the house for another month, he finally came outside.

As he tried to live with what he had done, life still went on. Somehow, we had put this madness behind us. Still eating at me was the purse, and something told me to go back and search it again, which is what I did. Well, still, it was empty, and it felt just as heavy as ever. I felt like it still had something hidden in it. So, I ripped out the lining, where I found a bundle of $100 bills, which totaled $5,000, tucked inside.

Stuffing the money in my pocket, I ran home, telling no one I had it, not even my mother, brothers, or sister. I hid it until I spent it all. I spent what I needed here and there, on the house and on my brothers and sister. Once that was gone, I went back to what I knew best and started selling drugs. Still unsure if I was good at it or not because all I did was sell enough to buy myself something to eat; I wasn't yet going after the big money. Drug selling was something I was just experimenting with for now, but I remained the strong-minded kid who was out to be successful.

In the hood, if you wanted to make money, it wasn't in the sales of cocaine because the drug of choice at the time was PCP. So, I picked up a bottle and went to dipping, looking to find America's dream. Coming across the PCP was easy; I just didn't have any sticks to dip in it and didn't know where I would get any.

This was when I went to the five-line lot to see if I could get my first dip sale off, taking some three days to make my first sale. You could tell I was a first-time dealer who learned to get into the swing of things. By the end of the week, I was a full-time dealer, dipping PCP with the best of them. The first thing I learned was not to get high off my own supply, as I wouldn't let PCP or any other drug pass my lips. This started me out in the right direction of being a drug dealer. My first experience didn't turn me into a full-time drug dealer because I was still in my robbery stages.

Learning from the OGs, I got to watch them dip and go, which taught me a lot and showed me the tricks and trades of the game. With money exchanging hands, the supply was being demanded. While the teachings went on, all I had to do was learn how much I had to deal with, how much water to put on the stick, and how much money to collect for it. I was selling everything from nickels to 30s, which is what the whole stick went for.

To me, as it made dollars, it made sense. Make no mistake, I was learning a trade I didn't even know I wanted. Now, along with my robbery spree, I was in the business of making people's problems go away. Thinking I was a healer didn't help; as the pharmaceuticals flowed, I flowed with them, all the while making a name for myself.

Still, after a long day, I would go home at night to my family and get a good night's sleep, just to wake up and try my hand at drug dealing again. As they say, there was enough money to go around. The OGs didn't see it that way. Wanting all the money for their sales, they couldn't get enough, so they chased me off. Now I was sneaking to sell my drugs, which was getting harder and harder to do, but somehow, I managed. What little I was getting was helping me, even though it was very little. And since no one told me that I should be seizing the opportunity while it lasts, how was I to know that in the drug trade, the opportunities wouldn't always be plentiful?

Chapter Seven:
Red Runs Deep

Even after learning to sell drugs, I still loved going to school, with my grades still being up. I was now being graded in the hood, where I wasn't coming across any failing marks. Just as in school, my grades were up, so were they in the hood. By now, I felt I had come a long way in my learning. School was everything to me, and I wondered how long this would last. I went faithfully, but from time to time, I would get a break and take trips to places like Venice Beach. I remember one such trip, going to Venice Beach, where I wore too much red to the Venice shoreline crab hood. Crabs came out of the woodwork to see who we were, and we felt like we were in the fight of our lives or we were going down. Outnumbered by the crabs, it was time to get out of there, and as they gave chase, we ran.

Running in all directions, we headed back for the car. Finally, everyone met up at the car, and we jumped in and left. All the while, heading home, the Blood homeboys wondered how these crabs knew we were Bloods. I didn't know if I should tell them, it was because of me, and I came to the conclusion that I wouldn't say anything. All I could think of was how I got lost and tried to find the car. Not knowing the streets at all, I was only happy because the Blood homeboy ran past me, and I noticed him running. He was someone who knew his way around the streets of Venice, and as he guided us back to the car, I was happy that I ran into him. Otherwise, I would have been running blindly through the crab neighborhood. But for now, we were safely headed back to the hood with everybody in tow. Remembering that we were still heated, the Blood homeboy said, "Y'all wanna get back at these crabs?" Without hesitation, it was on.

That's exactly what we did because we had guns on us. The only reason we didn't carry them on the beach was because we didn't want to risk getting them taken. With the two-to-one ratio of crabs to Bloods, we needed our guns at all times. There was no way we were getting caught without them, knowing LA was strange like that. If you didn't know they had a gun, you assumed they did because if you had one, you packed it, staying ready so you didn't have to get ready. That was always on my mind - all a part of the game that the streets played.

I remember how happy we were when Blood and I made it back to the cars, but we did not have the keys to get in. I used my Nickerson garden skills of how to break into a car to get in without being noticed. Blood grabbed two guns and handed me one, just to be on the safe side. Meanwhile, we waited for the rest of the Blood homeboys to reach the cars, ready to shoot any crab that would rush us if they saw us. Luckily, no crab did.

As the rest of the homeboys made it to the cars, we got locked and loaded. On the drive back to the hood is where we did our most damage, as we had thought earlier that we would go looking for the homeboys who hadn't made it to the car yet. However, everybody started showing up, and we didn't have to.

As we sat in the car, revenge was the only thing on our minds. Pulling a couple of blocks away from the beach, we opened fire on some Venice shoreline crabs we saw walking. Without waiting to see how many would drop, we drove away. We stopped at every red light so as not to draw attention to ourselves. I must have been paranoid because it was taking forever for the red lights to turn green. I just wanted to get out of the area before the cops could get on to us.

Seeing cops headed in the opposite direction toward the scene we just left didn't help the paranoia. But looking casual, we just drove on, and it seemed like whatever casual-looking meant, it worked for us. Both cars split up as we took different directions back to the hood. We didn't even imagine who we could possibly run into on our way. It was none other than a car full of crabs. They nodded at us like we were crabs, which made us feel a certain way, pissing everybody off. We couldn't help but think, *what do we do?* We sped off, leaving nothing but casualties.

As no one was the wiser, we headed toward the freeway and headed for home. Riding in silence, contemplating what had just taken place, we finally made it back to the hood in what seemed like no time at all. Upon reaching home, we got ready for a BBQ, which went off without a hitch. From that day on, we went on with our lives, never to hear about what had become of the crabs we had shot up. The next day, we were back to school.

Remembering my track and field days from 112 St. school all the way to Markham Junior High, I was happy about being in the gang-banging capital of America. I told myself that I was never leaving Los

Angeles, and I mean it. But who was I to know that? I was just a kid, not knowing where life would lead me next.

As my attendance and grades were up, I was missing school less and less and getting into fewer troubles. It was probably because I was actually in class, studying and learning. This year, I studied more than any other year, and it was reflected in my grades. Doing this, I thought I was going places. But living in the projects, doubt always came into play in my mind. However, I never once blamed Nickerson Gardens because I had a love for the place. So I just dreamed of, thinking back to my track and field days at 112th Street School. Only one person could beat me, the homegirl from Belhaven, but at Markham Junior High, no one could beat me. Still, I had no dreams of sports being a way out; I stuck to my academics.

Sometimes, the only way for us to get a meal was by going to school. But earlier, going to jail over the summer got me put on probation for the first time. I received my first mean probation officer, who didn't have to emphasize my going to school because I liked going to school anyway. I'm not saying there weren't any missed days or there wasn't any trouble, because there was. It wasn't out of the norm because school was a place where normal seemed to be the only thing that made sense.

At school, my friend from the other side even made me see crabs in a different light. Moreover, he did enough by himself to the point I thought that it was the only good thing about crabs. We would sit together in two or three classes, talking about each other's hood and flirting with girls, having nothing but fun doing our work together. Yet, I still had to go home, where all wasn't great on the home front.

As my mother spent more and more time with the dope fiends on Avalon off of Belhaven Hood, located in a crab hood, my big brother

73

began to follow her, eager to spend time with her even if it meant playing with the dope fiends' kids. The homeboys didn't understand; they only saw him hanging out in the crab hood and began questioning his loyalty to our hood, asking why he wasn't there with us. This situation turned dire for him. This led to him leaving the hood forever ahead of time, saying goodbye to Watts and Los Angeles without his family. But he had to go because the homeboys were willing to hurt my brother, so he made the difficult decision to depart and start anew.

Moving to Phoenix, AZ, with our family, my brother had to go for the first time without our very important mother. Graduation was fast approaching, marking the start of summer - a season I would come to hate for the rest of my life. Situations were more dire than ever; after school, one day, I learned we were being kicked out of the projects because my mother was too into drugs to pay the rent. A month later, we received the eviction notice. But before then, graduation finally arrived.

For the first time in my life, I felt nothing could stop me. Graduating from Markham with all A's, I was given a plaque for being the most turned-around kid, affording me the privilege of every parent at the school wanting their kids to take a picture with me. This was my first accomplished feat, making it the first time in my life I was proud of myself. It took my mind off all the problems at home as I walked across the stage with honors.

Once that was over, we went back to the grave reality as we were being kicked out. I had to face the thing I had dreaded all my life, as I never wanted the thought of leaving Nickerson Gardens to cross my mind. However, now it was unavoidable. After staying another month, my mother was asked to move in with the dope fiends, at least until she found another place, which she did. When she came to collect her kids, everyone moved out except me. Refusing to leave, I remained in the projects, where I stayed with our belongings. The project, no longer ours, provided shelter for about two weeks as I clung to the idea of staying in Nickerson Gardens. Little did I know, leaving Los Angeles altogether meant my days there were numbered.

Having to leave the only home I've known for the last 15 years broke my heart, so I rebelled against leaving. I ran away from home to the only place I've known, the Nickerson Gardens, where my mother knew exactly where to find me. Hiding from her for a day, I started to commit crime after crime to go to jail so I wouldn't have to leave Los Angeles. But it seemed like I just couldn't get caught, as my mother loved me too much to leave me behind. She finally found me in the five-line lot and forced me to come with her. It was a sad day for me, contemplating what I would do. At first, I thought about running until my mother gave me that mean look of "you better get in this car." So I held my head down, looking like I wanted to cry, and got in the car, knowing these would be my last days in the project. This is when I found out we would be moving back to Phoenix. The next day, we were at the Greyhound bus station, where I learned that it wouldn't just be me and my siblings. We would be taking an additional child. My mother informed us that she was pregnant with my little sister by my stupid stepdad. While I was happy for the little sister, I was mad it was by him. Throughout the journey, I briefly considered bolting for the hood as a way to escape the situation. However, I did not want to break my mother's heart, so I ultimately stayed. Boarding the bus, I could feel my heart breaking. Truly, this was the saddest thing I had ever done.

Before leaving, we headed to our old project and packed up all the clothes we could carry, along with a few blankets, and then we were out. We left behind all our furniture and anything we couldn't carry. I remember all the goodbyes. I can recall hearing my homeboys telling me, "You will always be from the hood; don't worry." I tried to hold my head up, believing them. They threw me a going-away blood bash, which somewhat lifted my spirits. Still, I cried as the bus pulled away from the station. I just didn't want to go.

While we were on the bus, a fire ignited inside me, driving me to return to Los Angeles and Watts. This burning determination consumed me as I sat in silence, tears streaming down my face. Reflecting on past events, I realized I should have seen this coming. A year earlier, my aunt had moved her family back to Phoenix, and I remembered how miserable she had been. That should have been my first clue. However, the intensity of this fire within me didn't fully register until we reached Phoenix. Throughout the journey, I couldn't sleep, dreading the direction we were heading - away from the safety of the hood. But there was no turning back now.

After 6 to 8 hours, we arrived in Phoenix. Standing next to the bus, waiting for the driver to unload our luggage, my tears turned from sadness to hate. Now, in the city that had robbed me of my happiness, I began to rebel. I resisted anything and anyone who stood in my way. Despite my mother's insistence, I reluctantly grabbed some bags and dragged them slowly behind my family. Lagging far behind, I secretly hoped the bags would tear up. That's how intense my anger was over the fact that we had to leave Los Angeles. When my mother warned me about the possibility of me tearing the bags, I defiantly continued at my slow pace. I thought to myself, "I don't care. Do whatever you want to me."

Leaving the bus station, I momentarily lost sight of my family as they rounded a corner. For a fleeting moment, I considered dropping the bags and running for the first bus headed toward LA. But then I realized it wasn't a practical idea. Eventually, I caught up with my family, and I heard my mother instructing me to wait right there until she returned. She scolded me, warning me to stop acting up and to keep up with the rest of them, threatening consequences if I continued to misbehave. She said she'd give me something to pout about if I didn't quit acting like that. Defiantly, I retorted that I wasn't planning on staying anyway, secretly resolving to run away and return to Los Angeles at the first opportunity. As my mother walked off toward the phones to make calls to family members for assistance, I couldn't tell if she hadn't heard me, didn't want to deal with me, or perhaps understood my pain and chose not to respond.

By the time my aunt picked us up, I was still in a rebellious mood, unwilling to listen to anyone. As we piled into the car and headed for the South side to my other aunt's house, I remained silent. Once we arrived, I didn't speak to anyone as I entered the house. I just sat on the couch as tears slowly rolled down my cheeks, contemplating the situation I was now in. Exhausted from not sleeping on the bus all the way here, I quickly fell asleep. In my dreams, I imagined still being in the hood, only to wake up to the nightmare that I wasn't. It was a horrifying realization, and I struggled to come to terms with this new reality.

As the sun was still out, I couldn't discern the time of day amidst the turmoil in my mind, fueled by hate. I was ready to explode on anybody, including family. So, I chose to spend the entire day sitting outside alone, avoiding interaction. After hours of solitude, I reluctantly returned to the house. At that moment, my aunt, seated in her wheelchair, beckoned me over and asked if I was angry about leaving Los Angeles. Though I remained silent, I nodded in agreement. Despite the upheaval caused by my mother's decision, I was taught to have manners and respect, which I tried to uphold. That night, as I ate, I still contemplated running away despite feeling a sense of happiness at being reunited with family I hadn't seen in a while.

I started to think that if I couldn't be in Watts, I would bring my Watts attitude to Phoenix in a way that would never be forgotten. After finishing my meal, I went back outside and sat alone until well after dark, reminiscing about LA until it was time to go inside and sleep. As darkness enveloped me, I fell asleep, only to awaken with my Watts Los Angeles mentality as the sun rose over the horizon. Despite the new day, I still didn't feel any better; in fact, I was now more mad than depressed. Not knowing what depression was, I couldn't be anything but mad. Yet, now I was too enraged to even cry. So, I watched my tears dry up.

If my brothers and sisters were mad, it didn't show. Maybe they were just too young to understand where we had just left. However, I fully understood what they failed to understand, and nobody wanted to be in Los Angeles more than me. Although I felt the need and urgency to go back home, I was already at home, and it seemed like I was there to stay. Nonetheless, it still did not feel like home.

Still feeling rebellious, I walked outside to hear this dude say, "What's up, fuzz?" But, he had used the C word.

Instantly, I went into defense mode and went off on him with "What's up, blood?" I told him I ain't no crab. "Don't be fuzzing me," I said angrily.

As I scared him, he turned and ran, calling for his big brother, who was from the other side as well. I didn't realize that I had scared the little brother of a childhood friend until his big brother came out and greeted me by calling out my name. While talking to him, I told him that I hadn't known that I had been talking to his little brother. "My bad," I said apologetically.

From there, a friendship blossomed between me and someone else from the other side, and we became the best of friends. I entered recruit mode, aiming to persuade my new friends to join the Bloods, those who would have it. Once we straightened everything out and they left, I began to wonder. Would I run into an evil that's hiding out in the hardcore streets of Arizona? So I set out on my path to see - to see who would resist me and who wouldn't. Believing that resistance was futile on my path to righteousness, I sought my bliss to navigate through this world.

As I started hanging out with my homeboy from the other side, he introduced me to people throughout Arizona. I got to know more and more individuals. That's when I learned there were no Bloods in Phoenix. However, since I had gone there, I knew I was about to change that, becoming the first Blood in Phoenix, AZ. This was the soundtrack of my defiance against my enemies. As my homeboy and I roamed from the South side to the East side to the West side, I met and befriended many new people whom I could call Homeboys. However, by initiating the rise of the Bloods in Phoenix, AZ, I was placing myself in the midst of a war zone. With the other side engaged in their own conflicts, they now had to take on a new enemy.

I knew there would be plenty of time for other endeavors, but then I started hearing about this market where drugs were sold. Therefore, I decided to walk there to confirm if it was true and what they claimed - that one could sell weed and cocaine at this market. Upon arrival, I realized it was indeed true. I observed people running back and forth, chasing down customers and cars to sell drugs. Witnessing all the hustlers and smokers piqued my interest. Adjacent to a pool hall where gambling was prevalent, I began to think it was the ideal place for me to establish my presence in the drug trade. However, I made a conscious effort to steer clear of the pool hall, which served as a front for gambling, as I didn't want to risk becoming addicted. Nonetheless, I occasionally observed others gambling, though I refrained from participating myself.

Because my mind was fixed on how to get some money to enter the drug game, I liked the way money was exchanged in the market. There were young and old people gambling alike. I began to wonder how the market and pool hall could have so much money circulating. Instead of jumping in headfirst, I took a step back to observe how the money flowed. I realized that rushing cars would be my best way to make money in this environment. There was plenty to be earned in the Third World. Not knowing exactly where my money would come from, I knew I had to get into the game. So, the Third World became the place where I could put all my learning and teachings into practice.

Chapter Eight:
Rising From Watts

Although I was still missing Los Angeles and longing to return to Watts, I knew I had to get used to my new life in Arizona. Upon heading home to my aunt's house, I was angrier than ever. This was because we were made to clean up the front yard despite not having made the mess ourselves. In an act of rebellion, I tried to talk back, but my uncle, who didn't like that, got in my face. He told me I better get outside and clean up. Disliking his command, as soon as I opened the door, I took off running. I considered that an act of running away from my new home. This time, I was more determined than ever to get back to LA. Despite both my mother and my uncle screaming for me to return, I kept running. I didn't know my uncle, who had been looking out for me, was coming after me. He didn't run, but he still caught me. He tracked me down at the corner gaming stop, where he snatched me up and punched me for a little while before making me go back home. I headed back with my head hanging down. Finally, I made it back home.

The only good thing that came out of it was that I didn't have to clean the front yard. With my uncle being a thorn in my side, I could no longer openly rebel against my family. I knew I couldn't let it show, even if he wasn't around. If I did anything rebellious and he found out, I'd get a smack upside the head. To get around that, I rebelled in the streets, with an attitude to terrorize anything and everything; I just didn't care. After all, reality wouldn't let me get caught up in imagination. Therefore, I set out to paint my name as an OG in Phoenix, AZ. I knew my goal wouldn't come easy by any means necessary. Gunshots were promised to me, and I promised myself that I would fight forever. Starting out without a Dad and lacking certain things only fueled my anger, and the madder I became, the more I felt the drive to survive.

Growing up, acting out, and behaving badly became a survival tactic of mine. But first, I had to master the hustle game. So the next day, I headed to the market to see what I could come up with. As nothing was coming my way, I realized I wasn't going to pick up anything tonight. Therefore, I went home and woke myself up from my fantasy. I realized I was no longer dreaming about getting paid. The realization sparked a fire in my spirit. I put on my "do or die" suit to live as living proof that I wouldn't be scared. I was a Blood from Watts, so I flamed up, putting on my all-red suit with red chucks to match. I never felt like I had to run in my red suit, so I wore it everywhere. This was the start of my journey in Arizona, where I asserted myself as a Blood, representing all the way from the Watts Nickerson Garden projects.

With all the red I was wearing, I was increasingly getting noticed by everyone, both crabs and non-crabs alike. Although everybody and their mother were trying to discourage me from wearing so much red, saying there were crabs out here who wouldn't like that, I didn't care.

I was here to go against the grain. However, there was one Crip who didn't get on my back about wearing so much red. He was the only one who stood by me. He didn't care what color I wore, and it gave me a reason to think that I didn't have to hate all crips. For a while, he was the only Crip I showed respect to.

While we lived in a crip neighborhood, the crabs of the neighborhood couldn't stop me from being who I was. I roamed their hood with my head held high. Eventually, I started saving money and slowly entered the drug game by selling marijuana first. I bought 100 joints dirt cheap, then turned around and sold them at a profit. This was made possible by me and my homeboy breaking into our first house together, where we came up with items we sold for a profit. The older neighbors we knew became our main clients. Back at the market, sales were going well, and the more weed we bought, the more weed we sold. However, we didn't realize that we were only making enough money to get by. Times were changing, and we had to grow up and change with them.

This was when I met my first homeboy who wanted to be a Blood like me, adapting our style. He asked if he could hang out with us, and he never went home since, forming the first of our three-man crew. From there, the crew would grow much bigger as we became known as a mix of Bloods, Crips, CC riders, and Gangstas. Later, these people became my Blood brothers in the family. At that time, it was the right moment for us to become family because crack had hit the scene hard, becoming the drug of choice. I jumped in headfirst, trying to make as much money as I could.

The real money started coming in, so I dropped the sales of marijuana altogether, understanding the principle that you don't get high off your own supply to make money. Saving up from the proceeds of marijuana sales, I bought my first stack of cocaine powder. I went to one of my uncles, who was deeply involved in the game, and he showed me how to rock it up, from cutting it up to the process of making crack.

As soon as I hit the block, I was initiated into the crack game with my first three crack sales. After that, I sold out, making more money than I had ever made from selling weed. So, I bought an even bigger sack of cocaine powder and learned how to rock it up. I discovered I was good at selling crack cocaine, and I was on the block every chance I got.

As I was making so much money, I stacked enough to buy my first car while still in high school. Things had drastically changed since Markham Junior High School. Now, here at South Mountain High School, I was no longer getting all A's. I was ditching classes more often just to drive my car or go sell crack. Additionally, I found myself staying up all night at the all-night clubs.

Around this time, I met my first girlfriend in Arizona, who later became the mother of my first child. It was around 2:00 or 3:00 AM when, after talking all night, she asked me if I wanted to go home with her. Not wanting to hesitate, I said yes. As I went home with my first girlfriend in Arizona, we spent the night making love for the first time. I dated her exclusively for a while. However, I ended up catching my first case and went to jail while being with her. During that time, I learned that she didn't want to wait for me, but I did find out that she was pregnant. Despite everything, we remained friends after I got out.

At this time, I met the most beautiful girl in the world. At least, she seemed so to me. I found her so pretty that I just had to have her, even though I was dating her best friend at the time. But I was mostly into her, so I didn't care about keeping up with her best friend. Finally,

I got my opportunity one day while picking her up from school. We became inseparable ever since. Though it took a little longer for us to make love, I remained patient until that time came. When it did, we gave it to each other good, which made me stay with her longer than I had stayed with any other girl. But all good things don't last.

Soon, I also ended up going to jail for her too. Surprisingly, she stuck with me throughout my time in jail and even after I got out. After a few years, she became pregnant with my second and third child. Now, I found myself wondering what I should do. Should I turn around and go back to jail again? But before that, let me tell you about how I met the mother of my third child - she was the first girl I fell in love with. I couldn't let her go, and we enjoyed spending time together. In fact, she ended up giving me my fourth, fifth, sixth, and seventh children. At this point, I had two baby mamas, and I was still with my third child's mother, making me a two-baby-mama daddy and boyfriend.

However, after being together for many years, my third child's mother finally left me, but not before I met my fourth baby mama, who ended up giving me my ninth child. Now, I found myself in a three-way relationship, juggling relationships with three baby mamas at the same time. It took some time, but eventually, my third child's mother called it quits, leaving me with two baby mamas once again.

Due to all the hustling we did together, we eventually got caught and ended up in jail again. It was during my time in prison that I met and fell in love with the only other girl I ever loved. But guess what? I couldn't resist adding a fifth baby mama to the mix. Now, I found myself handling relationships with four girlfriends at the same time. It somehow made me feel like a man, having one girlfriend and three baby mamas. What more could I want?

Knowing that they knew about each other wasn't a problem - at least not in the beginning. Life was moving along, and I was handling my business, still trying to be the big man in the streets. Eventually, I found my stride, hustling more and more until I was filling my pockets with cash at the end of each day. Two of the four girls hustled with me, and we turned it into a game, seeing who could rake in the most money and challenging each other at every turn. We pushed ourselves to the limit and beyond, making so much money it was almost shameful, but we felt no shame. We sold to every smoker who came our way while my two baby mothers pursued their own hustles, each being a go-getter in her own right. The competition between them alone was enough to keep me on my toes. Somehow, though, they knew that it wouldn't be enough, so we pushed harder, striving for even more. I knew that the more I pushed, the harder they would go out and get it, all in the name of love. These were strong women, one stronger than the other, who would change my life forever. But, as I said, we got caught. Finally, we were taken away to face charges. Everyone pleaded guilty, and we were sent off to separate prisons to prepare to do our time.

Our first time doing time was when I learned that loyalty doesn't always lie here. Well, I mean, I had loyalty from my two baby mamas, who were locked up too. They were in the same predicament as I was. But the other two were out as soon as the handcuffs were put on, off chasing after the deepest pockets. It didn't make me mad, but I couldn't help but think that they could have told me they were in it for themselves. They got out a few years later.

Once I was out, I was back to my old tricks, getting back down to the hustle, which I learned I was still good at. Then I met her, and I just lost it – one of the women. I fell head over heels in love with her. It felt good to have just one girlfriend, and I let her know that I loved her to the fullest, showing her every step of the way. She would be mine, and indeed, she became mine. As we played together, just the two of us, she fell in love with me. For once in my life, I realized I wasn't dreaming; I was actually living a reality of love. It lasted a few years, just me and her, inseparable.

Then came the return of Baby Mama, fresh out of prison, stepping right back into my life. I was faced with an option, and guess what I did? I took on a girlfriend and a Baby Mama again. For some reason, I couldn't, wouldn't, or didn't want to let my Baby Mama go. So, I found myself living a double life all over again. This time, though, I was determined to make it work. Being good at what I do, I regained my money status, known as being street-rich. I even bought and decked out a car for myself, which only enhanced my reputation.

Back at Third World, I was back on the block, hustling once more. Yet, my Baby Mama still tried to run a competition to see who could bring in the most money, and I loved her for it. Third World was my playground, where I had all my fun money-making days, surrounded by friends and my Baby Mama. It had been quite some time since I left school, and now I was trying to live on my grown man's tip, taking care of two households, which kept me out of trouble.

By now, I had let go of thoughts about returning to Los Angeles. I would visit here and there, but Phoenix, AZ, was now my home. I had built a reputation for myself, earned a name, and formed a gang that I was running. I was going places. Now, I was hustling in the early hours of the morning, even hitting up after-hour joints despite being too young to get in, but still finding my way inside. By now, I had brought my homeboys into the game with me, and we were running amok in the market and those late-night clubs, raking in so much money that we only went home when the sun came up.

However, one particular morning, I didn't head home straight. Instead, I decided to take a detour to my girlfriend's house, who would soon become the mother of my child. As I stayed there, I ended up falling asleep at her house only to wake up to some breakfast. After spending a wholesome morning together, we started making love and continued that all afternoon. I remember thinking to myself: *How could she possibly not become my baby's mother?* After all, I spent most of my time having sex with her. Thinking back, I recalled the day when we made love for the first time. At the time, she was a virgin, and that night, I knew for a fact that she was mine. After making her bleed from busting her out, I went to work between her legs, which brought us closer to the process of love-making.

Later, she officially became my first Arizona girlfriend. Whenever I went to the block, she would come with me. She'd sit and wait for me while I stood there all day making money. As long as she could be with me, I felt happy. That's what she liked to do as well. But my first girlfriend experience wasn't what I thought it would be. We didn't have that spark of love at first sight. Despite not feeling the love, I stayed with her. Then, a month later, I found out she was pregnant. But even as I learned I would become a parent, it didn't bring us closer.

As I started to date other girls, I came across the most beautiful girl in the world. She was so pretty to me that I had to have her, so I chased her until I got her. By then, my son had been born, and his mother and I had long broken up. I focused all my attention on the most beautiful girl in the world, whom I met through her friend whom I was going out with. I knew I would be leaving her for her friend, and I didn't even think twice about it. Though it took some time to wear her down, I finally won her over.

Our relationship developed from there. I tried to buy her love as she made me feel at home with her. In the beginning, she showed me her love. A year later, my second son was born, but I wasn't there for the birth because I got locked up. Spending two months in juvenile detention made me miss out on seeing my son being born. After the baby was born, I vowed to see the next one. After making love to her for a week in different ways, we found out we were pregnant again with number 2. This time, I would be in the delivery room.

Watching my daughter being born was magical, and it became something I would never, ever forget. Walking out of that delivery room with my head held high, I went right back to hustling. After all, I felt I had to buy my baby girl things that she would need to grow. So I put in the hours while my baby momma was in the hospital. Then, a few days later, while things were going so well, she walked into my life. Something told me this was love at first sight.

As I got to know her more and more, I realized I wasn't in love with my baby mama; I was more infatuated with her looks. After all, she was the most beautiful girl I'd ever seen. When she walked into my life, I made her mine, and my heart started beating faster that day. I held onto her for decades, wishing I could have held onto her forever. I still remember the first night we made love. Boy, how the sheets were wet when we were done! Even though I didn't know I could do that, it was amazing. I remember thinking, "This is me, looking at her, meeting her." By morning, we were at it again, and she looked just as beautiful. She was like no other person I'd ever seen. To me, she was the one that made the sun come up, and I couldn't wait to rush to the market to see her every day.

Not only was she the best girlfriend, but she was also a hustlerette, and I loved that about her. She was the hustlerette in all the right ways without being a streetwalker. I felt so happy and proud that she was mine – every part of her. What she had between her legs was mine as well, along with her. As I was a little possessive and the jealous type, I refused to share, and she wouldn't give it up for anyone else.

A few years into my two relationships, I ran into the second-best hustlerette, and she was second only to my girl. She wasn't from Arizona. Instead, she came from the land by the coast over to get her hustle on with her brother, who had brought the product. They added me and her to the mix, and together, we made a lot of money. We branched off into the neighborhood, opened up shop, and brought in more money than I had ever seen in my life.

As I was getting my money from her and her brother, along with making money by myself, my money tripled in no time. It was coming in three ways as it was supposed to, and we lived like this for a few years. And then, it happened. I started sleeping with her sister, and all of them became my baby mamas in one way or another.

Eventually, I ended up in jail again, and it all came tumbling down. Once I was freed, I picked up where I left off. After I returned, I was down to two women again. This did me no good because they weren't here, and it felt like I was a bachelor again. Although the cats were away, the dog continued to play, but she was always on my mind. I had to see her, so I found a way to get to where she was. When I first saw her again, I knew I was still in love with her. So I kept coming back, trying to win her over again. I kept telling her that I had never given up on her and that I still loved her. It seemed to work because I even bought her a radio and TV and made sure she had money on her books.

I wanted nothing more than to have her, so I still played the field until I met her. I did that until I felt that feeling I hadn't felt in a long time, or even thought that it could happen again. This time, my heart didn't just skip a beat; it was like I was soaring through the sky. I sat back, eager to see where this unexpected flight would take me, constantly wondering how she managed to take me on this incredible journey. Staying true to her, I still found myself following her. It was like she was transforming into the one I was deeply in love with. How could I love her more with all my heart when I already loved her with all my heart? Plus, I was still waiting for her. It was like my heart couldn't beat without her. How could it beat her, though? Now, thinking about it, why does my heart seem to beat with two rhythms? I wondered if I was in love with her as I was falling in love with her was incredibly confusing in the beginning. Then she got out, leaving me, and I had every intention of leaving her for the one I truly loved. However, my heart wouldn't stop beating for her and also for my other girl, so I walked the thin line of both, torn between two loves that seemed to define my very existence.

So, I was now playing two sides of the field. Balancing these relationships was tricky, but I managed to keep both going. I hustled with her but not with the other. However, I mostly served with my homeboys. Not only did we hustle, but we also had fun at times. We would bet on who could drink the most alcohol. The stakes were simple: drink until you pass out or lose your money. The homeboy pool was growing, and we had more new friends than ever. This led to wild nights where we bonded over our shared love for hustling and drinking.

After everybody got drunk and couldn't walk anymore, the only homeboy who wasn't drinking had the unenviable task of lifting everyone up and putting them in the car. He drove us home carefully, ensuring we all got back safely. Once home, we stumbled out of the car and into our respective beds, where we slept off our drunkenness.

The events of the night swirled in our hazy memories. Those nights were a blur of laughter and the unspoken bond that formed between us as we navigated the highs and lows of our chaotic lives together.

Chapter Nine:
Chasing The Game

The next day at the market, I ran into this big-time baller who had a group of friends who were also big-time ballers. When word got back to me that they were looking for workers to get rid of that product, a few of my friends and I hurried up and jumped at the opportunity. They started fronting us ounces, which took us to the next level of hustling. This is when I started being stingy to myself and everyone else, as I was putting in an effort to save my money. Watching it stack, I saved enough to buy myself a few ounces. Hitting the ground running, I got rid of my dope and his dope, and finally, I was starting to see some real money.

At the time, I still had the same car, and it was time to buy another one. This time, I got a two-door and something fast. Boy, how I loved that car! It was big enough that I could put my girl and the other girl I had started taking an interest in in the back seat at different times. When I bought that car, I forgot all about my first car. I never drove the four-door big boy again. I didn't like the way my money went down from the purchase of the car, so I went right back to hustling, trying to make up for the money I spent.

I also wanted a motel room just for the night to take my girl. I would go home to her later, but first, I was out to make some money. So, I worked the market late into the night and didn't think about getting the room until the morning. As I took her to the motel, we entered and came out determined to never let this go. Then I went right back to hustling; through which I now had stacked enough to have a nice little nest egg, making it grow by the tens of thousands. I just let it run up.

Eventually, we got the good news that we were pregnant. I had a baby on her, and she forgave me, but she was mad that she forgave me. One day, sitting in front of her house, I met my next best friend, who became my brother. Even though we kind of bumped heads when we first met each other, as both of us were ready to do each other in, and me being with a few of my homeboys scared him. He was ready to take us all on if we didn't get off in front of his house, or should I say spot. But we decided to let bygones be bygones, and we became the best of friends. All of us formed the hustling pack. Everybody would keep the money they made, while I would put mine up for a rainy day.

As the world started developing around us, we felt like we were developing with it. So, we invaded the east side to sell our crack, opening up a way to make more money. I was putting it away by the boatload, and despite my young age, I felt more mature than I actually was. If only I had been more mature, thinking I knew what I was doing! No, I didn't know what I was doing, and being headstrong didn't help. But at that time, I was living without any hurdles in my way, so I just started spending instead of investing.

Still, right then and there, I had been around a lot of girls and started messing around with my girls. I was fully aware that I was still in love with both and not knowing who I loved more only killed me. They weren't okay with it, and they were already struggling to deal with each other. Even though I knew bringing in another was breaking the rules, I did it anyway. I didn't do it for money or anything like that. I did it just to get sex because I had money. Playing that game, I played a lot of girls out of their panties. Though I was doing the wrong thing, I still didn't stop, and I kept hurting her and my other girl.

It wasn't intentional or anything like that because I never wanted to hurt either of them. I knew what having a broken heart felt like. Still, I couldn't get over the New Girl, and I wanted to get between her legs. It seemed like I had to meet the new girl. I was still going home between two households, but that was nothing compared to what I'd seen. I never thought this could have been me, but I just couldn't get away from my bad habits.

Nothing made me more money than serving on the street behind the market. I knew it was more dangerous. Smokers would come through in their cars and drag you pink with road rash, asking for a large amount of crack. Most people would rush for the car, where the smoker would slap all your dope out of your hand, and you'd try to jump in, getting caught in the car, to where you'd get dragged pink. I watched a friend of mine go through that, thinking if I had been a second quicker on the jump, that could have been me. He went to the hospital and never returned to the streets through no fault of his own because the streets will break you just as fast as they make you. I watched a lot of people come and go. The thought of death and the violence on the streets would prove to be too much. It seemed like another normal thing going on, so I bunkered down, determined not to let the streets take me under.

Living through it all, I prospered. Around this time, everybody started hanging on the back streets, leaving the market alone for a while. Not that it was getting hot; it was already hot. Everyone saw how secluded it was on the back streets to hide from the police, which caused my profit to go down. But I still worked the block, and since I wasn't making as much money, I stayed later and later.

Knowing people were slapping crack out of dealers' hands to drive off with it, all the drug dealers had a surprise for the next person who tried it. Wouldn't you know it happened the next day? This time, the person doing it got their car shot up, causing them to lose control and wreck it. That's how it goes when you have a lot of guns on you. Watching as the ambulance came and took them away, we learned they had been hit by some of the bullets. That was just another day in my neighborhood. Dreams wouldn't come that night. How could they when no one was getting anything? Plus, dreams were few and far between these days. This is where things started to go wrong. With the back streets getting hot from all the shootings and drug sales, everybody decided to move back to the market, where selling drugs made more sense.

Now, after selling all their household products on the market, they were getting down to the nitty-gritty, and this is when they came in with selling their guns. They had only one rule: buy every gun you can so it won't be the gun that kills you. This is where my arsenal started to grow.

Then, in stepped the Los Angeles boys. They were a bunch of gang-banging, drug-dealing killers who mainly brought their drugs to Arizona to sell. With Arizona being a state where you could get more money for your product, a lot of them were Bloods, but most were Crips, who were set on making money. They thought they could take over the town, which led to more killings and more drug addiction, shooting the crime rate skyward. The cops didn't know what to do until they created their own gang squad called the Gang Squad. So, not only was it us against them, but it was also us against the cops. And even though the cops mostly went after them, they still came after us whenever they got the chance.

If you throw in the Arizona crews that tried to come after us, I would say it was us against them and us against the world, which is the way we liked it. Bring on all crews, and we'd take them down, which is what we did, facing every adversary every time. Being brought up like this was a test of the neighborhood, where my homeboys and I were protectors and fought for what was right. We still did our wrong, but we tried to make up for it the best way we knew how.

For instance, my cheating was still going on. One day, I saw my girl at the park, and guess what she was doing! Beating down some girl she thought I was trying to hook up with. That made me want to take her right then and there. As she was the type of girl who would let me, the situation was even more interesting. Though I waited till we got home, then showed her. We made love in some of the hottest ways. She was ready for anything, and she took me all in. This is where I was able to appreciate her opening up even more. After all, I opened her up.

Yet still, the other girl was on my mind. I couldn't stop thinking about her, and nobody wanted both of them to be happier than I did. So, I kept trying to make them happy. Knowing I had two girls I loved made me happy, and it just kept growing in me. Not only was this how I wanted to live, but this was how I wanted it to be. Living like this had become my way of life. Though I was running around doing my thing, the game was starting to get good again. The hustle was back on, but now everybody was shooting at everybody.

The time came when we had to defend ourselves. With so many people getting shot, it was crazy. So, my crew and I picked up our guns. It had now come to the point that we were shooting back, too. We came close to being shot by what we would find out were some LA boys who did a drive-by on us. We jumped in our cars and chased them, ending up in the back of the homeboy's El Camino. As we pulled up to the lights, all hell broke loose, and gunshots rang out. Bullets were flying in every direction, even hitting a fire truck that was passing by.

Thinking on his feet, my homeboy threw the car in reverse. As they took off, we then took off after them. The cars getting mixed up had put us in that predicament. We didn't know we had pulled up right behind the shooters. Now, back at the market, safe and sound, on watch-duty for any more drive-by shooters, we assessed the damage. Seeing a bullet-riddled car, we realized how close it came to our driver being hit, which would have given them the drop on us. With no one being hit, we went back to our regularly scheduled night.

Prior to this, we had found out that three people had been hit in the drive-by earlier and had been taken to the hospital. However, everyone had survived. There was no time to waste; it was like the game never skipped a beat. As no one fell out of step and all the money kept coming in, it was just another night in the city with everyone taking their chances like a roll of the dice, hoping not to get caught up in crap. Despite the chaos, nothing stopped, and nothing halted. That insanity was in full swing more than ever, and everybody was determined not to miss out.

Now more closely involved with my family, I didn't want my brothers and sisters in the game like me, but it was too enticing for them. Ultimately, they joined in too. Initially, they were not on my level, but as first-time beginners, they did well. Entry-level was a little bit harder without money, so they got started the best way they knew how with their allowance. They guided smokers to the house as if they had their own spot, which brought money their way. As they were trying to get on my level, they looked up to me. In no way whatsoever could you tell them that I wasn't big time. Who had kingpin status? I often thought. I was just an OG from the projects, only dreaming of making it big.

Eventually, the Los Angeles Crips were getting out of control. After committing another cruel act of shooting, it was clear the situation was escalating. Two friends and I loaded the car with guns and went looking for them. Instead, we ran into the police and got pulled over.

Our attempts at hiding the guns went in vain because the police still found them, along with the extra clips and all the extra bullets we had. Driving around like this, we all were taken to jail. They got released, and I was taken into custody and sent down. I was released three months later and returned to the madness. This time, I was on parole, which didn't stop me from jumping right back into the game.

Once again, I thrived, but this time, my mind was set on building the future. So, I put away every dollar I could get my hands on. Before long, I was buying half birds, going from rocks to half ounces and even more ounces. Hearing "you the man" made me want more, so I turned whatever I could get my hands on into birds and advanced as if I was "hood rich." As hood-rich as I felt, it had perks - it brought new panties to play with. New girls came only because I had money, which wasn't a problem for me because I only wanted one thing: what was new between their legs.

As I was good at taking them on, it was the only thing that kept me repeating my actions. Sack chasers were the best find because I didn't have to worry about anything. Everything would happen within the first night of our meeting. This is what I always liked in those girls - I didn't have to deal with them later anymore. It excluded every possibility of heartbreak. I had no heartbreak with newbies at all, knowing only the two of my girls had the power over me to do that. Up until that point, I had never had my heart broken.

My mother taught me to watch out for girls. Now that my mother had her next baby, my little sister, our family grew to six brothers and sisters. After that, she went on to have six more kids, bringing our clan to 12. In the beginning, life was good, and we tried to stay tight-knit, thanks to the closeness my mother instilled in us. We welcomed our little brothers and sisters into the family with the utmost love and open arms, and they knew they were loved.

Growing up, we weren't like any other family - we weren't normal. There were rules for others, but to us, there were no rules. Going to school, we often took things to another level. We made friends, but nobody wanted to mess with us because of our friends and the family members we were related to. Known for being roughnecks, we were tough on the other kids. We played rough, and if you weren't tougher than us, you had to be tough to play with us. I always tried to be the toughest kid in the world, and I wanted my little brothers and sisters to be just as tough. We taught them how to be strong, and naturally, beating up the bully worked in our favor.

My girl – I could always remember how she loved my brothers and sisters. She knew them all personally, and this shows how far back me and her went. Even today I would say that she knew me best - always knew what was going through my mind. I often found myself thinking about her, with no malice in my heart for her, for my other girl, or anyone else.

My family was my world. I never wanted to see my brothers and sisters get hurt or come to any kind of harm. Being the second oldest, I played the role of a big brother and protector. I looked out for them at all costs, ensuring their safety by trying to take over the streets. As I was known as the person who did all those things on the streets, it didn't take long for me to become known as a killer. It didn't matter whether I wanted that reputation or not. It was just a sweet misunderstanding, and I decided to run with it. As my reputation grew as one known for violence, I made it clear: if you didn't touch my family, you wouldn't have to find out if I was one. I let it be known to everybody.

One day, while I was at my girl's house, her mother came home from working at the market. It was a place where a lot of drug deals went down. Though she lived just one block away, it was another area rife with drug deals, with people constantly running up and down the street chasing cars or, rather, their customers.

I remember seeing how her mother got mad at seeing all the drug dealers hanging out in front of her house. She quickly ran inside, grabbed her .357, and ran back outside, squeezing off a few rounds into the air. Though she scared nobody, she certainly got everyone's attention. All those who knew the cops would be coming decided to flee the scene, while all those who didn't know were forced to deal with the cops when they arrived at the scene. Her mother accomplished her goal of getting rid of the drug dealers for a little while, but she knew they would be back. That taught me something important: her mother was the meanest yet the nicest person one could meet! She was truly afraid of nothing.

Though now I was well acquainted with her daughter, we moved from one corner to the next. Although we were across Main Street, we were still within walking distance of the market. This allowed her mother to walk to work.

One day, after the cops had chased everybody off, I arrived late and didn't know what was going on. As I wondered why the market was empty, a car pulled up with customers wanting drugs. Specifically, they wanted the drugs that I had on me. Without thinking, I rushed to the car. But at that same moment, I saw a police car turning the corner.

As soon as I took the money, the cops sped up to rush me and the car. I took off running as soon as the cop opened his door, but he remained hot on my heels. As he continued chasing me, the cop car pulled over the car I had just served. However, I didn't stop and kept running for dear life with the cop on my tail. He was just about to catch me when something unexpected happened. Luckily, the cop tripped over something and fell, giving me the chance to escape to my girl's house. She opened the door and let me in, hiding me from the cops. By then, they had a backup arrived and started searching for me.

Being safe and sound in her house, I had nothing to worry about. I thought about how close I had come to going to jail. Once the scene had all but dissipated, I didn't return to the market that day. Instead, we decided to go to a motel and get something to eat. That's when our utmost love-making came into play. Despite not even going down on each other yet, it was incredible to make love to her in every possible way. Imagine something being exactly picture-perfect; that's how it felt like being with her. She seemed like a dream come true. I felt as if it was just me and her in a perfect world.

The next day came, and the magic of our time together ended as reality set back in. I headed back to the market to sell my drugs, but I remained excited all the way. Just knowing that my girl and I would pick up exactly where we left off, made me giddy with happiness. After waking up the next morning, I recalled the events of the night before. I even got laughs at how the cop fell while chasing me. Things were back to normal; I got my money like nothing had happened the day before.

But the reality of the situation was far more bleak. I had to go back home to my other girlfriend, who wasn't the girl with whom I had spent that memorable night. In fact, months had passed since my great night with her. It was during this period that I first experienced going down on a girl. However, my first time wouldn't be with her.

Though it was with another beautiful girl, it was a beautiful experience, too. I remember when she asked me if she could do it to me, the heat of the moment led to me doing it to her. I didn't know what I was doing, but I gave it my best and tried to emulate what I had seen. She wasn't a pro, but she was better than me. Stiff and hard afterward, we made love. From then on, this became a part of our sexual routine. For a while, she was the only one I was doing that with.

A few more months passed before I did this with anyone else. Though she never brought it up, we both knew it was her turn. So, I took it upon myself to bring it up. Boy, every time we did it, she definitely got into it and enjoyed it. We talked about it but didn't go straight into doing it. I just didn't let her know when I would be doing it. She just knew I would, and this anticipation made it all even more fun.

After that night of bliss, I knew it was back to the market to make more money. With everything going well, I decided to let my guard down at times. One day, an undercover cop suddenly came to the market to buy some drugs. Everyone knew she was undercover, so when she tried to fool us, one of the homeboys got mad and ran up to her, punching her in the face. She must have hit some kind of panic button because cops came from everywhere, pulling up just in time to save her and catch my homeboy in the act. They quickly placed him under arrest and charged him with aggravated assault on a police officer. We wouldn't see him for nine months.

This incident started a trend for the whole crew. Everyone started following the homeboy to jail at different times with various charges. It became like a revolving door - nobody wanted to go, but it seemed like as soon as one got out, another went in. A few months out on probation, I caught another charge. Determined not to go back to jail, I led the cops on a car chase. Eventually, I drove home and got caught, ending up on even more intensive probation. I became one of the first candidates for this program, but I violated it, too, as I couldn't stay away from the streets.

How could I stay away? I had to get my money. So, I went on the run, only to get caught down the line. Since it was my time to go in, one of the homeboys got out. It seemed like none of us could be out at the same time anymore. I thought this trade-off to jail had to stop, but it didn't for a while - actually, a long while.

Anyway, I got out a free man, but had I really learned a lesson? No, I just found a better way to get around the law and jumped right back into the game. I became a monster, hitting on women left and right. They all caught some of it, but my girl took it the worst. Perhaps it was because I expected more from her, knowing that I loved her. For hurting her in that way, I apologize. I'm truly sorry. But I can't help but think about the times, like when I got out of jail, and she and her friend had that crack car. She saw me at the market and scooped me up, and I jumped in the back seat because she had the front occupied.

As we drove off, she climbed over the front seat and joined me in the back. We started playing around, and I played hard to get, but she was having none of that. She just took it out and started riding it right there in front of her homegirl, who was driving us down the street. That turned me on so bad. I was happy to have a freak. However, dealing with life on a day-to-day basis was a trip for me.

Chapter Ten:
Battles Beyond Bars

Living my life on the streets was rough. I didn't have it easy, with everybody looking up to me and depending on me. This was all because of how good I was at selling dope. I didn't want to let anyone down, so I tried to help them all - every last one of them. This pressure pushed me to sell more and more drugs. It forced me to grow up faster, knowing I had to take responsibility and become an adult.

However, this path led me to jail one more time as a minor. I got sent back to juvenile prison and had to sit in the violators' yard. A week later, I went before the parole board to find out how much time I had to do. They told me I would be sent to a boys' home placement.

The boys' home was a cozy place tucked somewhere in the woods, complete with a barn. I thought I would stay there and do my time. There were no bars or barbed wire, but there were calisthenics. We had to complete a running course, which meant running a mile in a certain amount of time after coming home from work since it was a work camp. We did work like building trails through the Grand Canyon. On weekends, they would take us mountain rappelling, white water rafting, and doing other activities of that sort. Surprisingly, it made doing time actually fun. We even had visitation rights. I was looking forward to seeing my mother this coming weekend.

When the weekend came, my mother didn't show up, and I felt disappointed, thinking I wasn't getting a visit. As it got late, I didn't expect a visit at all. But just then, guess who showed up? It was my girl and my little brother, pretending to be my aunt and brother. They got permission from the staff to visit with me. Guess what we did? We ran straight to the barn and started making love to each other while my little brother kept watch. I knew that what we were doing was prohibited, and it turned me on even more, which prolonged our love-making session.

When we finally got off together, I was very satisfied. After putting my clothes back on, we just sat there talking. She kept trying to persuade me to get in the car with them, but I knew that would have put me back on the run, so I kept refusing. As the visit came to an end, inexplicably, I chose to stay. For the love of me, I did not know why.

But as soon as the next day arrived, I went on the run, escaping from the placement facility. The day before, I could have accepted a ride, but instead, I took off through the woods until I came upon a river that thwarted my attempt to cross it. Following my instincts, I turned away and headed toward a mountain, eventually spotting the main highway about two miles away. I trekked toward it and reached it by nightfall. Reluctantly, I hitchhiked, and after a few cars passed me by, a man in a white truck picked me up. Initially fearful, I soon realized he was a religious man who simply wanted someone to preach to. He generously drove me all the way to the next town, where he dropped me off at a store.

Seeing a sign pointing towards my hometown, I started walking down the highway towards it. This time, I got picked up by a Native American. He offered to take me all the way home if I accompanied him to the Native reservation, to which I agreed. Two hours later, I arrived in my hometown and began searching for her, going through the homeboys to find her. It was late in the early hours of the morning, and the town was deserted with no one in sight.

Remembering where my homeboy's girl's mother stayed, I went over to her house. She directed me to where my homeboy stayed, referring to him as her daughter's man. When I arrived, I was surprised to find my first baby mother staying there. We ended up reconnecting that night, sharing a moment, making love on the couch that we both knew would be the last time. By morning, she had left again.

Now, all my attention was focused on my girlfriend. I was eagerly anticipating the next time I would see her. I tried to concentrate on our relationship and spent the day with her in my homeboy's room. He graciously let us have some privacy because he knew how much I cared about her. We spent the entire day and night wrapped up in each other's arms in his bed, making love. We did it about four to five times that day and continued making love into the night. The next morning, I woke up feeling like I was on cloud nine.

But as the hustle continued, it was back to the streets as usual. Soon after getting a sack, I was back to making money, adding to the pile I had saved up before I went away. However, it seemed I was headed back in sooner than expected. One day, I went to the courthouse to visit a friend at court, just a few months after my release. My homeboys joined me, and we started eating sunflower seeds in the courtroom, casually spitting them on the floor. We caused a ruckus, disrupting the court proceedings, which prompted the guards to intervene.

Upon seeing the mess and noticing me with a bag of sunflower seeds hanging from my pocket, the police asked me to step outside the courtroom. They questioned if I had made the mess and ordered me to clean it up. When I refused, they attempted to force me to clean it. In response, I resisted, and they rushed me, handcuffing me in the process. I tried to fight back, but they forcefully brought me back into the courtroom, bursting through the door. What I witnessed next shocked me.

As the judge jumped up and ran for his chambers, they entered with a Taser and used it on me. It dropped me to the ground immediately. They continued to chase me until I was finally under control and in handcuffs. I was then hauled off to jail. After spending one night there, I was released back to the streets, where the hustle was still going strong.

So I dove back in, head first, buying myself a nine-piece and opening up shop. It quickly grew into half a bird, causing money to flow in steadily. After several months, I had to return to court, where I was placed on adult probation for the first time. It was part of a plea bargain that I accepted willingly because it meant I could stay free - free to make money, free to roam the streets, and most importantly, free to make love to them - to every new one I could encounter, but mostly them, my girls.

As the money rolled in, we were making more than ever, selling ounces like it was the thing to do. My brothers and sisters had the east side covered, and I fronted them my stuff while I worked the south side. She was also involved in the drug sales, making it a trifecta of sorts, and I felt like the winner. However, everything changed when I violated my probation and went on the run again. The money was too good to give up, so I took it in stride, running for as long as I could. But the game had changed; turning 18 wasn't a guarantee that things would be alright. I managed to avoid getting caught for a while, stacking my money as I went, unaware of how little time I actually had.

After finally getting caught, I ended up in county jail for violating probation. Unable to secure a bond, I had to wait until my next court date. They offered to reinstate my probation with five years, or I could take 2 1/2 years in prison. I quickly turned down probation and opted for prison time. It felt like no time before I was inside, getting my prison number and assigned to a minimum-security yard. Determined to establish myself, I soon realized my street reputation had followed me into prison. Here, I encountered the political dynamics of prison life for the first time.

Though the yard I was in was filled with your average convicts, where everybody had a short amount of time, their equality played on the race card. I only got involved where my involvement was needed, but after a year and nine months, I got out. Once again, it was back to the streets, where it was time for me to play in the hustling game again. Mostly, I was thinking about how I was going to play with them. Though I was on parole for the remainder of the 2 1/2 years, that didn't stop me from jumping back into the hustling game.

When I jumped back into the hustling game, this time, I could work my magic with my half a bird. Putting on some size by hitting the weight pile, I came out swole and looked good with muscles in all the right places. Now, thinking back, I can reminisce about my first riot in prison. It happened because the administration tried to change up and reduce the food. So, we burned whatever would burn. This was the only time all the races had ever come together since I had been going to prison. We had to sleep in a barbed wire closed-up gated cage outside overnight in the freezing cold. Finally, the next day came, and we were let back into our respective dorms. Most of us were asked to pack up and head for lockdown.

Of course, I had to be one of the people going to lockdown, where I spent nine months fighting for my freedom to get out soon or lose my good time and remain in prison. Finally, my chance to speak to the board came, and I won my case. I was then sent to a different minimum-security facility from lockdown. A few months later, I was released. There I stood, right in the middle of the thick of things. Even though it was hard, I made it look easy. I dipped my toe back into the hustling game and went into it full-blown after that.

The only thing that got me down those days was the fact that my homeboy had died while I was in prison. He was killed over this gang-banging situation brewing in Phoenix, AZ, with Bloods against Crips and Crips against Crips; it was going down hard at the time. Though the homeboy was killed by a Blood, the Blood that did it was also killed about a year later. Though he was the first to die a violent death by gunshot wounds, he certainly wouldn't be the last. As my love grew for the Eastside Homeboys, the crew got a little bigger. About a year or two later, I lost another homeboy to gunshot wounds, leading to another violent death by gang-banging. This time, a neutral Eastside homeboy got killed.

However, this time, I got out to find out more than just the gang-banging situation had changed in my life. Getting out, I found out that the woman I referred to as 'All Beauty' wasn't my girlfriend anymore. She left me for all kinds of dudes until she settled on one. When I met another girl, she took my mind off 'All Beauty.' It was like we hadn't even had a relationship. So, I put my heart into her, the new girl, and my other girl, concentrating on them mostly for days to come.

I wanted to get some things off my chest, so I went to see All Beauty at her mother's house. However, her mother told me she wasn't home and that she was at her auntie's house down the street. This is where I found out she wasn't my girlfriend anymore. I walked up to her and her new boyfriend, kissing as I came down the street. But upon seeing me, she ran up to me and gave me a kiss and a hug in front of her boyfriend. I thought maybe I had a chance with her, so I tried to talk her into going out with me to give me some. But she wouldn't budge. She said she couldn't get away from her boyfriend.

Later, at one of her family gatherings, I ran into her sister, who also gave me an embracing hug and kiss. When the get-together was done, I got together with her sister and made love to her. The next day, I made love to All Beauty as well because she was able to get away from her boyfriend. We made love in every room of the house because nobody was home. Thinking I had just been with her sister didn't stop me from doing what I had to do. I had to have one more shot at that.

Once done, I couldn't help but think that before I went to prison, I had her, All Beauty, and the one from out of town all pregnant at the same time. They gave me three kids in the same year that weren't even triplets. The one I referred to as Out of Town wasn't too bothered by it. Letting that go, she took my dope game to a whole new level, showing me how to take dope out of town and set up shop in other people's hoods. This brought in more customers than I thought was possible. More money was spent because drugs were hard to get in their town, and selling out in a matter of hours was nothing for us. We would drive back into town, get more drugs, and drive right back out. Now All Beauty was a thing of the past, and I was now out of town with my Out of Town baby mama, hitting the quad factor, which was money coming in from four different ways: from me to her, to out of town, to my brothers and sisters.

With me constantly going to Eloy, I didn't have time to spend my money, so it stacked up. In no time, I made $30,000 to $40,000 in a matter of weeks. Well, up on a chicken, I bought my first bird. This is where she found out I was doing it with All Beauty's sister. As I kept lying to her, letting her know I wasn't, she figured it out when she and All Beauty's sister got into a fight. Ultimately, the circumstances led them to all find out that I was doing it to her for sure, and she had no more doubt in her mind.

She finally put two and two together but found out Out of Town had been out here before selling dope, getting caught with nine ounces in a chest area in a bra. After bonding out, she ran back to her out-of-town state, where she waited a few years before coming back to Arizona, still having a warrant for her arrest. She was arrested and charged with the nine ounces, receiving six months and some probation for the charges.

For now, we were still going out of town with our drugs. Once, something felt wrong to me, but I didn't follow my instincts. Consequently, a jacker tried to come in and jack us, asking for $100 worth of dope. So, I pulled out my sack. Handing me the $100 bill he had, he grabbed the sack and ran with his gun, not knowing all I had in the sack was $100 worth of dope, causing him to pay for what he tried to rob. I'm glad he didn't shoot me when he stuck the gun in my chest. We packed up and went back to Phoenix, gunned up, and prepared to go back to the small city. But first, I had to go through the tragedy of losing my uncle.

With Crips doing what they do, one of them shot my uncle, supposedly all in the name of the homeboy who had been killed. They demanded to shoot the next person (anyone) who would walk through the door in vengeance for the homeboy dying. This is what this Crip did, killing my uncle as he was the next one through the door. Living day-to-day is what we did in the hood, especially with the Los Angeles gangs converging on Phoenix.

This was where gang-banging took a turn for the worse. Bloods were riding down on Crips, and Crips were riding back. It now had everybody riding down on everybody, causing gang-banging to be at an all-time high. Eventually, it became obvious that they needed the city to do something about it. More and more gangs moved to Los Angeles. They were mostly Crips, but it was all the Bloods who were bringing in all the dope. They brought in more cocaine than a city would allow. This blended right in with the drug trade of Phoenix, moving off the south side to somewhere on the west side.

During this time, we grew to love the next out-of-town homeboy who became family. He was from the Midwest, bringing that Midwest vibe to the group. Now, with all the new faces, it was time to quote some Bloods in. So, we went to the projects and quoted her little brother, her cousin, and a few other people into the hood.

With the hood growing in Arizona, we knew that Hunters would be known. That day, we called it a night, and the next day, it was back to the grind. The homeboy hooked up with his baller chick, who introduced him to jacking. He then taught me how to do it as well. He had a target he needed to rob, so he took me with him. We ended up robbing the targets for a whole kilo of cocaine. Along with the money and jewelry we got, we made off with a substantial haul. Once back at my house, we split everything evenly. I ensured I got half of everything, which amounted to 18 extra free ounces of cocaine, plus some money and jewelry.

I took the haul to her house and explained how I got it. She didn't believe me at first, but I convinced her. Gang-banging and drug dealing were closely connected. I would head to the west side to sell some of my dope. Only two or three Crips knew I was a Blood, so I blended in with the others who were unaware. After selling the dope, I would return to the hood. The hustle was understood: get that money by any means necessary. Though they tried to jack me in Eloy, I didn't stop going to the small town. This time I just went back armed and dangerous. We were fully armed. The next day while in Eloy, the so-called jacker showed his face. So I confronted him, not caring how many times I struck him, squeezing off the whole clip. Then I tried to post up in the spot like nothing happened, getting surrounded by what seemed like a thousand police at the time.

They didn't care that we had a key of dope in the house, hidden of course. They only searched until they found the guns, taking me to jail for the first time in the small town. I bonded out the next day, which was easy since all I had to do was see the judge to set the bond. I went right back to the spot where they had just been and set up shop again. It was rolling; we didn't want to shut down, serving tough for about a month straight.

Then, I had to go back to court. Pulling up to the building in a candy apple green BMW with gold leaf that read "BIG DADDY KANE" caused the whole town to think I was a big-time baller. Walking into the courtroom, they tried to charge me with aggravated assault with a deadly weapon. I was allowed to stay out on bond and went right back to hustling. After another month passed, I had to go back to court, only to find out this time that the charges had been dropped. As always, it was back to business. I brought one of my homeboys down from the city with me to the small town, and he quickly started cutting into their girls, taking some of the bad ones from their men. Some men, who couldn't go without their pretty faces, broke down and called the police on us on numerous occasions. This should have told me to get out of town, but I didn't.

A few days later, my little brother and I were pulled over by the police, and I was taken to jail for something stupid. All night, I was worried about my little brother. I got out the next day and saw he was fine. This still didn't make me leave Eloy alone. I knew I should've gotten out of town when taking their money didn't mean anything, but taking their women did. But I stayed, selling throughout the day and night, then heading back to Phoenix to prepare for the next time we came out to Eloy.

Before leaving, one of their main guys came to me and asked if I would front him an ounce. After talking to him for a while, I agreed to front him, telling him I would bring it in tomorrow when I came to town. The next day, I did what I said I was going to do, and he finally came and picked it up. That's when I knew I had made a mistake by fronting to him, especially when four days passed, and he still hadn't paid. That's when I went looking for him. At first, I thought about putting a bullet in him, but then I thought twice and decided to take it as a loss.

By now, the police were on to us, but we still didn't want to leave the town. I had no trust in anyone there. A month later, we were raided. All week, I had this feeling in my stomach that they were coming. So that day, something told me to take the dope and put it in the car. When they hit, they didn't find any drugs in the house, only in the car, and no one claimed the car since it was in someone else's name.

Still, the three of us in the house were taken to jail and charged with the sale of narcotics. That day, we saw a judge who gave the two women $75,000 bonds and gave me a $50,000 bond. We knew we were stuck.

The next day, we were transferred to a bigger jail, where I sat for two weeks until the charges were dropped. Going through hell, I had never been happier to hear that my charges were dropped. I found out that my out-of-town baby mama had gotten her charges dropped a few days earlier. Back in Phoenix, thanks to her, she picked me up in the BMW and rushed me back to town so she could have me all to herself. We made love for two days straight, letting off frustration I thought I was never going to release again. I really took it out on her.

After that, I couldn't wait to get back into the game because I could just hear the hustle calling. But first, about her: Thinking back to when I first met her, I was sitting in my brother's spot when she came in. Walking through the door, I was amazed at what I saw in her, not knowing she was messing with her family, who went to jail on her. This gave me the chance to shoot my shot once she came to the spot again, showing up just as my brother and I were throwing a weed smoke-out party. This is where you roll all the blunts out of a pound of weed you can get. We had plenty of blunts to go around, and the only rule was the first one to pass out gets socked up.

Though we must have smoked about 50 or 60 blunts between the four of us, her friend was the first one to pass out. It took about 20 more blunts between the three of us before she passed out. They were ready to go home, so I asked her if I could go with her, telling her she knew I wasn't coming for nothing. She agreed, and we gradually walked them home.

We headed straight for the bedroom. Once there, we got down to business. She took her clothes off, and I just fell in love. Well, once I made love to her, I knew she had to be mine, and I set out to make her mine. I took her from her man, who was family. When he got out, he put his hands on her for getting with me. I talked him down, telling him he didn't need to hit women, especially since I had long stopped. He never hit her again and let me have her. It was just me and her until she got out.

But where? I almost forgot about my Westside girlfriend, whom I cheated on with her. I still wanted her, thinking my Westside girlfriend was just a fling because I was waiting for her to get out of prison. For now, I was with her and loving every minute of it.

The situation was going well until one night my brother threw a party, and my Westside girlfriend and my new girlfriend were introduced to each other for the first time. They almost got into a fight until I stepped in and broke it up. After they finished arguing, my Westside girlfriend left. I took her home and made love to her all night. Going home to my Westside girlfriend, I woke up the next day thinking about her. Then I got dressed and went to her, using the excuse that I had to make money to get back to her. My Westside girlfriend thought I was going to hustle, but I would be with her.

When she asked me to meet her mother, I got scared because of the age difference between us. I didn't know how her mother would take me or see me as messing with her young daughter. But meeting her mother, things went off without a hitch as she instantly started to like me. After seeing the way I cared for and took care of her daughter, she couldn't do anything but like me. So, we hit it off, and she became like a mother to me.

Living with her grandmother, I finally got to meet her little brothers and sister. They took to me right from the jump and became like my brothers and sisters. I introduced them to my son from my out-of-town girlfriend, whom I had custody of because she was in prison. Once they met him, they grew to love him as if he were one of their own.

After seeing him riding in the car with me to drug spots and doing drug deals, they told me this wasn't the life for him and asked if they could keep him at their house. I fell in love with her even more for wanting to raise my son as her own, seeing the lifestyle he was living wasn't for a kid. I said yes and let them take him, quickly putting him in school. They got him ready and off to school on time. My son paired up with her sister's son, and they became best friends, inseparable as they played together.

Now, it was time for them to move into their own place. Finding an apartment in the avenues, they took my son with them. Naturally, I came too, but I didn't move in. I spent my time living with her. It was she who had my heart; she had me blinded from the start.

Now that the time came for her to be free, she was released from prison. And she is who I ran to. Picked up by her cousin, she was taken to a motel, along with my two daughters. When I finally showed up, my two daughters were fast asleep in the other bed. So, she and I climbed into the other bed and did our thing, doing it two or three times that night. She showed me how much she missed me, playing hard to get until I got her to loosen up. Then, it was on nonstop. Not waking up our daughters, we had a good time, and I spent the night with her all night, not going home. We made love one more time in the morning before our daughters woke up. After we finished, they woke up. I played with them for a little while, then I went home. She

119

was very mad at me for not coming home. Hearing that she had gotten out, she knew where I had been.

But now, anyway, the homeboys were older, and we weren't hanging out as much. Though we would see each other around the spots in the hood every day, we were now doing less and less as a crew. We had to part ways. Now, I was in my own little world, and the homeboys were in theirs. We'd always come together, though, when the homeboys had a beef against someone.

Like when beef brewed against these crabs and my homeboy, who was also a crab. All because he was balling in their hood, and they wanted what he had. The leader of the crab hood and his homeboys tried to jack my homeboy, taking it upon themselves to shoot him in the chest. After losing two homeboys to gun violence, I didn't want to lose anymore. While he was in the hospital with a gunshot wound to the chest, they told us he would survive. But where they did wrong by us, it was on sight ever since that day. They knew they had crossed the line. Messing with one of us meant messing with us all. Now that the shooting had brought us all back together, we wouldn't let any of the homeboys out of our sight, always going somewhere in pairs.

Though we were now living a life of drugs, hustling, gangs, and guns, it led us to expect shootouts everywhere we went. Like the time on the freeway when we spotted those fools who had shot our homeboy. We had to let the bullets fly because they started shooting at us, too. Bullets flew, hitting the cars of innocent bystanders. It was shocking that no one was hit. After getting away, they must have planned retaliation all night because they ended up shooting up the spot, killing the next-door neighbor's son, the essay partner. Sometimes the innocent get killed, and sometimes they don't. Being a part of life in the hood, I learned a long time ago it was strangely this way, showing me true warfare existed where I lived my whole life. But the game is still called. I remember going to a Homeboy's house; he would rock up keys of dope in front of us. He took the powder, turning it into rocks and getting more dope than he knew he had, which was part of his plan all along. We went with him to drop it off to his workers; it seemed the right thing to do.

With killers trying to kill us and us trying to kill them, we knew we were safe in numbers. So when I started showing up later and later, the Homeboys thought I was getting soft or scared. This caused a lot of infighting, and when the homeboys and I came to blows because they tried to test my manhood, we ended up pulling guns on each other. Knowing we were all shooters, none of us were fired. We decided to talk it out before it went too far, settling our differences. It was all good again like we never fought in the first place. Making up just like that, all because I was spending too much time with my girlfriend. This had to happen, but as it made us inseparable again, I couldn't help but miss her. By now, I had moved with her and her family to a house in the mountains, where she and I had our own room—our domain where endless lovemaking happened. Reading between the lines, I knew the signs that I was only concerned with myself and mine during these times, and in this world of ghettos, peace was not part of mine. Knowing that couldn't stop the hustle.

As we went on this California run to pick up a couple of chickens, we jumped in the Homeboy's car. Being the only one with a license, I drove all the way, knowing we had about $50,000 or $60,000 in the trunk. We only went out there to cop because of the drought going on in Phoenix, and cocaine and crack were scarce. Once in California, we got a room and got some well-needed rest. The next morning, we called the California Homeboy to come get the money, but he didn't call back right away. So we went cruising through the city, driving by the Nickerson Garden projects, which felt and looked the same but had a lot of new faces walking around. I wanted to stop, but the homeboy said we're not here for that; we had other business to attend to. Eventually, the call came in for us to drop off the money. After giving him the money, he took off to get the dope. We went to the Slauson swap meet, knowing the homeboy would take hours to come back. We spent some money on clothes. While at the swap meet, some out-of-towners wanted to take pictures of us in our car. After taking the picture and putting the clothes in the car, we headed back to the motel. The Homeboys still hadn't shown up with the dope, so we decided to get something to eat. That's when we found out the water pump on the car was going out, so we pulled into a gas station in a Blood neighborhood to get it fixed.

While standing there, a car with two Bloods in it rolled by, eyeing us. They didn't see us at first, but then they rolled right past us just as the car went up on the lift. One of the Bloods walked past us and asked us what hood we were from. Without intimidating us, we just mean-mugged him. Not getting an answer, Blood reached into his pocket like he had a gun, which was even less intimidating because we had a gun too. Still not getting an answer, Blood gave a gesture, and out of nowhere, about 25 more Bloods surrounded the whole mechanic shop, asking us again what hood we were from. Acting like they were getting ready to rush us, the situation changed when one of the Bloods saw the out-of-town license plate on our car. Realizing we were out-of-towners, we told them we were from Phoenix, AZ, and that got them to give us a pass. Even though we were ready to defend ourselves, the situation didn't turn dire. Then, realizing we were all on the same page, they left. With the car ready, we paid the man, jumped in the car, and headed back to the motel, giving ourselves a good laugh. Where the homeboy still hadn't shown up with the drugs, we ended up spending the night in California.

But like clockwork, the next day, he showed up with three bricks of dope. This is where my homeboy and I got into a fight about who would take the dope back across the border. I didn't mind driving the money across, but I did mind taking three kilos because getting caught with those was a whole other story. Arguing that he had to drive them back made him mad enough to tell me I had to catch a plane back. So, that's what I did after getting my plane ticket money from him, thinking I didn't have to jack them for the car and drive it back to Phoenix.

Being the only one with a gun because they wouldn't take it back to Phoenix with them, I took the gun and went to the airport. I tried to check it in at the front counter but had no luck because I didn't have a lockbox. So, I took the gun outside and threw it in the bushes, went back in, bought my ticket, and boarded the plane for home. Once on the plane, I ordered some drinks and sipped my way back to Phoenix. I was no longer mad at the homeboy because I had beaten them back to Phoenix. As soon as I got off the plane, I headed straight home and went to sleep, only to wake up to the homeboys knocking on the door to see if I had made it home and to let me know they had made it back safely with the three keys in tow.

It was like we never got into it in the first place, making it back to business as usual. Going to the homeboy's house, we watched him put the whip on the three kilos of cocaine, turning them into 4 1/2, almost five birds. Getting back to the grind, we didn't run into any of our enemies and got no static. But here in the streets, where it was cold, you had to supply your own heat. So, I loaded up the AK and hit the hood, throwing it in the trunk with one in the chamber and the safety on. I was in the hood in no time, running into the homeboy who had just gotten out.

He didn't stay out long, though. He took a sack out and threw it on the ground right in front of the police, trying to tell himself they didn't see him. But they did. They quickly got out of their car, arrested him, and took him back to jail. He sat there for a few months, and I put my car up to bond him out, giving him a few months of freedom before he had to go back to court. In the meantime, he signed a plea bargain for 4 1/2 years, having to turn himself in to start serving that time. But the homeboy had other plans. He backed out of the plea, opting to stay out longer. By the time his trial came up, he skipped it, so they went on with it without him. They quickly found him guilty in his absence, sentencing him to 15.75 years until they caught him. When he was finally caught, he had to serve every day of it.

When things finally calmed down and got back to normal, another incident was always around the corner. We always had to be on the lookout for our enemies because it wasn't like we weren't being stalked by them. One day, while watching my back, my friend and I ran into one of our worst enemies, who was looking to gun us down. But he didn't know we saw him coming. Before he could squeeze off a round, we had already squeezed off ten rounds, riddling his car with bullets. More interestingly, we kept squeezing off rounds, causing him to jump into a field and crash his car head-on into another car. All this happened right here in the war zone, where the war was on. Not finding out if anyone had been hit in the car, we threw our gun in the trunk and drove off.

Finally, we got word that the leader of our enemy had been shot and that everybody thought he was dead. Upon his release from the hospital, he tried everything in his power to get revenge on us. Even though he was looking for us with everything in his arsenal, killing to avoid being killed was the way to survive. Managing to stay ahead of our enemies was how we roamed the streets. Still not being hard to find, I believed they were dodging us. While they lay low, months passed by, and I was still on the streets, knowing my days were numbered as I was wanted for the shooting of the said leader. Word had got back to the police that I was the shooter. Thanks to someone telling me, I would be caught and charged with attempted murder.

With Killer after us, we did what we could to stay alive, even if that meant killing back. I got arrested by a discriminatory officer who went off after I told him my name. He quickly pulled his gun, stuck it to my head, and yanked on me, trying his best to drag me through the window, aggressively telling me to get out before he shot me. Thinking he was going to shoot me, I stayed in the car until other officers arrived. I couldn't wait to go off on the officer who had his gun to my head, screaming how he discriminated against me and had a derogatory attitude. Ranting and cussing, I went off, with calmer officers trying to calm me down. I couldn't get over the fact that he stuck his gun to my head, so I made every fuss I could until I finally ended up in handcuffs, demanding and getting the opportunity not to ride with the discriminatory officer. Once at the station, I was still ranting and raving. Every time I saw him, I went off on him, knowing he didn't realize how he could have killed me, which made me even madder. But finally, processed out, I was shipped off to the county jail, facing 18 years in prison.

Finding myself in jail again, I couldn't get comfortable, thinking about what I was going to do. I just sat there, waiting to go to night court, knowing I wasn't going home. Three or four months later, I was waiting to go to trial. When my police report finally came, I read it and found out that the leader of the gang had picked me out of a photo lineup. Of all people, with as much work as he had put in, I never expected him to snitch. But there it was, in black and white, him telling on me. Still, I was ready for trial, thinking he wouldn't dare take the stand against me. So, I bunkered down for the long months and years ahead of me, now fighting off depression.

Chapter Eleven:
Visits And Vendettas

In those difficult times, I got a few visits from two of my girls, which kept me going strong. I wanted to get back to them. The person I supposedly shot this fool for was not thinking about me because I didn't receive even one money order or letter from him, and he was supposed to be my so-called homeboy. But if it wasn't for her and the other girl, I would have gone all the way crazy.

About seven or eight months later, while serving time, selling all those drugs finally caught up with the homeboy. The police started following him around, watching his every move and step. They showed him they were collecting evidence on him by pulling him over and finding the half a key they saw him put under the hood. They turned around and let him go without arresting him, which at first was a shock to him. A couple of days later, finally getting enough evidence, they arrested him. He found out they had raided every spot he had dropped dope off to, with people being hauled into jail with him that he knew.

Now in the same predicament as me, I only hoped he realized what I was going through. Still, I wouldn't wish jail on anyone. A day later, the homeboy was put on the same floor as me, but in a different pod, so we got to chop it up. He told me stories of the homeboys on the streets. As we settled in to do our time together, it was cool going to rec and kicking it with him. Plus, I loved the extra commissary I was getting from him. Having my own money, I didn't need his but took it anyway.

With five to six months to go before the start of the trial, I was more than ready to go home. However, going home wasn't in the near future. In those six months of waiting, nothing special happened, making it the most boring time I had ever had. Kicking it with a few of the swan homeboys and a couple of the i.b.g.d homeboys, where one of them became my roommate, was a blessing in disguise. That is until I had to go to lockdown for getting into a guard's face and telling him how I felt.

In a lockdown cell with a dude who didn't care about anything, I ensured that I didn't care either. They separated us and put me in a room by myself, which was cool with me because now I could think. All I thought about was what I would do when I got out, thinking if I ever got out. Finally, my trial date was upon me. Like I thought, the witness against me didn't show up, and I knew I was going home. With the case being dismissed, I was set free. This set the motion for me to be released.

Outside the jail, she was waiting with open arms. Still wanting to see her, I gave her all my time first. After a month and a half of being free, she found a job and wanted to move away from her mother's house, so I set out to back her play. Having the day off, we went looking for an apartment, finding one in a nice neighborhood. We moved in, meeting a few new homeboys came into play. Introducing them into the fold kicked off growth, causing the homeboys to grow.

Now looking to get back into the dope game, which grew into a whole new story. This time, we set up shop on the Southside again. All that was left was me getting a sack. Waiting till she got paid, I threw in what she gave me with what I had already, and I was back in a real way. This time, determined not to be stopped by anyone on my rise to the top. Starting off slow after about a week, the spot picked up. In a month's time, it was off and running. As word of mouth spread, more and more people came. Now, I was back in the swing of making money.

Around this time, my mother met her husband, who would go on to father six of my brothers and sisters, bringing our illustrious family to twelve. They met at a time when things weren't good. She got him to use crack for the first time. Still, we lived in harmony, as bad as ever. At a young age, we could make our own food and stay up late hours of the night. Sometimes, older kids wouldn't even come home at all. Still, we managed to get by until we could get by no more. Somehow, Child Protective Services got involved with my mother and her seven younger kids. She and my sister were forced into a position to do better with the kids.

At this time, crack had a stronger hold on my mother. She and my sister ended up losing my brothers and sisters. Once child support got involved, they stayed involved, and that was bound to happen. So happened it did. But our family went on. At this time, my mother had had enough of smoking crack and everything else. She checked herself into rehab for cocaine abuse. Finding one that would accept her, she checked in, determined to get off crack.

After not seeing my mother for what seemed like months, which it had been, I found out she was doing well and had been crack-free for a while, looking and feeling good about herself. When I first saw her at a job that I didn't know she had, I couldn't even recognize her. My brothers, sister, and I were so proud of her, making us feel like a family again. Knowing she had our backs and we had hers felt so good. However, she would have to appear in court to see if she would retain custody of my seven brothers and sisters. Finally, appearing in court, my mother found out she would lose all rights to her seven younger kids. To this day, I don't think my mother ever got over her kids being taken away from her. Somehow, she found a way to live with it.

After puberty, we went on to our community with no promise of a new day. In the hood, where life was in everyday life, times would be hard and getting harder. Now, taking family under my wing, I tried to keep him from going crazy and setting off into the world. I knew that by putting a gun in his hand, somebody was about to die. Though I couldn't keep an eye on him at all times, I knew I had to keep him away from the guns whenever he was around me. Away from me, he was doing the most, especially to become a real menace to society.

Going on about my life and still hanging with the homeboys, we decided to move our operations to the hooker stroll, where hookers would walk up and down the stroll selling their bodies. We set up shop in one of the hotels. Adding a new spot where all the Rockstitutes could come and get their rocks, turning tricks just to turn another one to get high. Pimps would even beckon our call, asking us not to sell to their hookers, mad because they were spending their money. Most of the pimps would stop by asking if we had seen their hookers. Their hookers would ask us to say they haven't been by, and most of the time, we would just tell them. Thinking, who were we to lie to pimps?

With the name of the game being cop and blow, the homeboy took it upon himself to start pimping. Having the rocks, he didn't have to worry about the prostitutes bringing the money back. Rushing us to get their high on meant more money for us. The only thing wrong with the new spot was that it had a lot of blind spots where you could run into the police with a pocket full of dope. That's exactly what happened to me. Knowing I was going to jail, something told me to walk right past the police. Doing so, they let me keep walking, so I hurried to my car, jumped in, and drove off. This motel wasn't as scary as New Jack City. The motel prior to this one had way more blind spots, where PCP was a part of our sales adventure. One of my homeboys took it upon himself to dip a stick and got high to where he got stuck on the 7th-floor balcony. Thinking he was going to jump, I had to coach him off the balcony before I could leave.

With PCP becoming a drug of choice for most of the city, it became a real money maker. Buying a vial of PCP at a time, it was nothing to dip a stick or two just to get high, which tested my mental state to the fullest, causing me to go into the mental hospital. Going to the looney bin, they would take me and tie me to the bed, four-pointing my legs and arms. Tied down, I was unable to move, all the while screaming delusional things. Trying everything in my power to get untied, but the doctors wouldn't let me up. After laying there for two or three days tied to the bed, the doctors would finally let me up and let me go home.

At that time, I didn't know the PCP was driving me crazy. I would smoke it and end up tied right back to the bed in the hospital. Sometimes, I wouldn't even smoke it; I would just pull on it to get it to run, which would cause me to go into a crazy state. But we got to the bottom of that, and it was no more pulling on. I wasn't even smoking PCP all because I knew I had to get out of my head.

Though that wasn't the only thing causing my mental state to stabilize, quitting it got me to calm down enough to let things go back to normal for now. Now was the time when both of my women were getting tired of my ways. First, one of them started seeing other people behind my back, telling me my ways caused her to be nasty. As for now, she was seeing another guy. Not long afterward, the other girl followed suit.

Catching her a few times didn't surprise me, but when she was unloyal, I never knew how to be loyal. After a while, I wasn't even hurt. Still, I messed around with her, pretending to fool each other with this "I still love you" crap. Though she didn't jump into cheating right away, I still had her, or so I thought at the time. Thinking I learned and lived with who and what she was, I also learned seducing men with her body was nothing to her. All I tried to teach them was how to be ladies, but all that went out the door after they started doing what they were doing. As they became nasty, they started doing it with anybody who would give them something, which caused them to get nastier and nastier.

Later, they became known as sack-chasing women, but I still couldn't bring myself to let them go. Both now loved when I went to jail, thinking they wouldn't get caught by anyone and have to put up with a fight with me. Most of what we fought over was their nastiness. Believing in it as I saw it with my own eyes wasn't the problem because they would bring me what they got from people, thinking that would make everything better.

At the time, not knowing if it did or not, only made me jealous, which still made them both mine. It only felt like I was holding on for dear life. Here is why I remember her picking up her first sack and becoming the down-hustle she was. She told me she asked my homeboy for a sack, which he happily gave her. Getting mad, I quickly made her give it back. Soon after, I threw a sack in her hand, and she took off from there, becoming a go-getter, taking the sack and selling everyone dollar for dollar, bringing me back all the money. This made me keep putting sacks in her hand. With her now bringing in money and me bringing in money, we raised the bar. But like they say, you can't turn a hooker into a housewife.

Knowing that's how she was, the other one, on the other hand, wasn't a hustler. Getting what she wanted as a flat-backer, she even tried to turn me into a trick. Teaching her that she deserved everything in the world because she was beautiful only sent her down the flat-backing road because she didn't know how to fend for herself as she did.

Now, with the hood going crazy from California hustlers and Phoenix hustlers hustling in the same territory, more and more bodies started showing up. You couldn't be caught in the hood without a gun, as the key was not to be caught slipping, like two of the homeboys that were close to me, losing their lives behind stupid stuff.

However, in this short time, that wasn't even close to how many friends I had lost, with the number being around nine or ten. As guns blazed a bloody trail, the homeboys and I stuck to our guns, mostly to protect our drug selling and to watch our backs. Doing what we had to do with what we had to do it with, the neighborhood being rough on us made us old before our time. Now, in this hood where dreams don't come true, we understand that it was us who were against the hood. Most of the time, the hood won, but we were married to the streets, and nothing could take us out of the streets. Nothing but a dream, that is. And since none of us dreamed anymore, we weren't leaving the streets. That wasn't the worst of our worries. Maybe we didn't want to leave the streets, as trying to live by the rules of the streets was doing no good, especially in streets that had no rules. Then you had the cops who handled damage control, claiming they were keeping the streets under control. They didn't know that dealing with what I was dealing with, you had to go through a lot. Believe me, when anything goes, you will go. Despite everything getting worse, things got even worse.

While living with her and the other one's mother, her mother met a problem, which got me involved with her problem. In the beginning, we weren't tight, but we were cool. Not knowing anything about her problem, I would talk to him, and he would talk to me on a friendly tip. All of a sudden, he had to go and show his bad side and start putting his hands on her mother. This was all around the time when her sons were locked up, so they weren't around to put their two cents in on him hitting their mother. At first, none of us knew he was hitting her. We still all moved in together and even blew together as he hid his hitting her from us.

After about six months of this going on, she got tired of him hitting her and called her daughter to come get her, who in turn called me, and I went and picked her up. Driving around, we saw her problem, and she asked me to tell him to leave her alone. Playing hero, I did so.

Pulling alongside his car, I told him to leave her alone because he was hitting her, and she was scared of him. Her sitting there, not saying anything out of fear, didn't shock me; it just threw me off. I didn't see what was coming next. He reached, pulled, and shot at the both of us, so I unloaded on him through the windows as he reversed his car. Turning around and chasing him, I unloaded and kept unloading until I could get him, but I couldn't get him right then and there.

She finally spoke and said, "I've been shot. I need to go to the hospital."

Looking at her, I said, "Me too."

Seeing the blood flowing down my face, she must've panicked, which caused me to lose my calm as well, not knowing how bad my face wound was. So I went to the nearest phone booth, called an ambulance, and ended the chase.

However, before the ambulance could get there, an undercover police officer pulled up on me. This was when I remembered I had an ounce of cocaine in my pocket and that I couldn't go to the hospital and risk them finding it. Now, with the undercover officer standing on the passenger side of the car, I snuck the ounce of cocaine out of my pocket and pushed it under the seat of the driver's side of the car. Then the fire department, along with an ambulance, pulled up. Given the once-over, we were taken to the hospital.

Finally reaching the hospital, they wouldn't give me any pain medicine, not knowing how many bullet holes I had in me. They took me and X-rayed me to see how many bullet holes I had in me. Finally, they came back with my wounds not being life-threatening. Having only a broken jaw from being shot in the face, they took me into surgery to prepare to fix my jaw.

After I woke up some hours later, I found out that my jaw was repaired, and I was sent to a recovery room. Going to the bathroom, I got up and looked at my jaw in the mirror. Seeing that my face was swollen to the size of a watermelon, that panic almost set in, but I stayed calm. Going to lie down; I watched TV that whole night. The next morning, visitors started coming, and nobody was prepared for what they were looking at, seeing me with my face so swollen. I kept assuring everybody that I was OK. Later, I got the news I was being released from the hospital.

Going home, I didn't know what to expect from my kids. They took one look at me and seemed confused, not understanding what had happened to me. Not knowing they were scared for me when I found out later on, it shook me to the core. This is when I knew I had to take revenge, or this fool would take me away from my kids. I couldn't let that happen.

After taking a month to heal, my face went back to its normal size. Months later, I still hadn't run into the fool who shot me, so I didn't think much of it and went about my life as usual. However, thinking about how my jaw was wired and how I couldn't eat solid food enraged me even more. This just turned him into my enemy and fueled my desire for vengeance. I was out for blood, though that would have to wait while I went through the process of healing. I was finally happy when the wires came out, and I could eat solid foods again. As days passed, I went about my everyday life, plotting my revenge. I didn't run into the fool for another year and a half, but I never forgot or forgave him for what he did to me.

One day, we happened to drive past each other, both throwing gang signs from different sides. I was out without my gun and didn't get nervous until he made a U-turn and started following us. I wasn't nervous for myself but for my girl because if anything happened to her, I would've gone crazy. He had shown he didn't care who was in the car with me when he shot me the first time, so I didn't put anything past him. I drove like a bat out of hell trying to get away from him, feeling relieved when I saw a homeboy who always packed a gun. I pulled up on him and asked him to use his gun. With that, I confronted the fool, who quickly drove away from the scene. I gave the gun back to my homeboy and vowed never to be caught without my gun again.

The next day, I took my gun and went hunting for him. I discovered him in front of the scrap yard, where I pulled up and opened fire, hitting him once or twice. My daughter, who was sleeping in the car, woke up from the gunshots. I patted her back, put her back to sleep, and told her everything was alright. Trying to act normal, I drove off and headed to my brother's house to drop off my daughter. I rushed to her job to drop off the car, distancing myself from the crime and any evidence. I thought, in case anyone saw what I did, I decided to take off walking to the bus stop. Jumping on the bus, I rode past the crime scene and saw my work being loaded into an ambulance. I rode on to her house, feeling assured I had gotten away with it, or so I thought at the time.

Finally making it to her house, I felt like I was in the safety of a shelter away from the police. I laid low, only moving in the cut, but it was hard as a hustler. I had to re-up and supply my spots. I didn't know if I was wanted, but the feeling of suspecting that I was wanted didn't help my train of thought. I knew I didn't want to get caught slipping, especially when I was out in the open. I avoided the police for about a year and a half, only running into them once and giving a fake name to get let go.

The day came when she had to turn herself in for some traffic tickets. Given ten days and a fine would squash them, I waited for her.

She got out a few days later, mad at the world because all her stuff had been stolen from her house. She blamed me, saying if I wasn't over her house, none of this would have happened. The only way to stop her from saying that was to promise to buy her new stuff. It came easily because we just had to tell smokers we needed new TVs and stuff, and we got new TVs and stuff.

However, this spot was getting hot, and it was time to move again to the safety of our relief spot, which would only take days to get going. Meanwhile, she got a job to tide us over. My day started off with dropping her off at work. I headed to the spot to sell all my drugs, which took a couple of hours. Selling out, I had to re-up. Re-upping, I headed for the new hideout to prepare the ounces for the spot. Little did I know I was being followed by the warrants and wanted a squad of the Police Department. Making it to the house, I sat down to cut up my dope and turned on the TV to watch the Super Bowl.

As I did so, there was a knock at the door. Not knowing who it was, I grabbed my gun and answered it. A lady on the other side asked for someone who didn't live there. I told her she had the wrong house and closed the door, returning to cutting up my dope. Suddenly, all the lights went off. Hiding the dope, I ran to the back window with my gun and saw a man messing with the power box.

Thinking he was trying to break in, I ran outside with my gun to check on him. Locking the door, I headed for a confrontation but never made it as the police tackled me around the corner, placing me under arrest for the so-called shooting of a Buster.

When they took me back to the house to search for the gun, I thought they would find the dope. Searching the whole house, they found nothing. After questioning me for about an hour, it was time to take me to the county jail, where I was formally charged. Sitting in the horseshoe, I realized I was facing serious charges. Seeing myself back in jail again was a killer, and I knew that once bail was set, I wasn't going anywhere.

After being sent to the side to dress upstairs, which took another 24 hours, I was finally sent to the second floor, where I had a lot of time to think. I went to my room and started thinking about what was ahead of me, only to think about the time the homeboy got killed at the club. In the middle of a shootout between two groups from different sides, as the guns broke out, it seemed like everyone at the club had guns. With people running and racing to their cars to get away from the shooting, bodies started dropping. Two South Side OGs lost their lives, and a few West Side cats fell. It was a bloodbath. Hot ones echoed through the ghetto, lives were lost, and only jail tested what was in the hearts of men. I saw no way out, but with everything weighing heavily on my heart, I sat in jail for eight months to a year, waiting to see if I would get 18 years or be set free.

This time, I went through no fights because no one wanted to test my fighting skills, letting me serve my time in somewhat peaceful skill mode. By now, the jail had started charging a dollar per meal, equaling $30 a month just to eat. Most fell behind on their payments but still got to eat. Any money that came in was confiscated before they could buy commissary, leaving many broke and making for a more miserable stay. Finally, my trial date was upon me. This was the place where we would tell it all, where the judge would make or break me. Around the time the trial was supposed to start, the witness didn't show up, which looked good in my favor. All the charges were dismissed, and I was freed from jail.

Chapter Twelve:
Cycles Of Despair

Getting out of jail, once again, I was a free man, but I still went back to crime. I picked up another cocaine sack to sell, feeling like I couldn't stop selling drugs. Hustling seemed to be in my blood. Freshly out, I was just in time to see the Millennium come in. Bringing in the Millennium with her was amazing. We celebrated at my brother's house in Coolidge with his family, getting drunk and having crazy sex. The new century was supposed to make the world better, but things in the hood didn't change. I was determined to build a brighter future by selling drugs for the next two years straight. My sister, brothers, and I sold dope, making it a family business.

Then, my sister moved out of my baby's mother's house into her own place, not knowing she was bringing herself trouble. She sold to an undercover cop at my baby's mother's house, then invited him to her new house, where she sold to him again. By the third time she sold to him, they were ready to charge her. The next day, the police came to her house and arrested her. She couldn't go to trial, so she and her attorney worked out a plea bargain for four to ten years, which she signed. She only had to do six out of the ten years, with the rest on probation. After six months in the county jail, she was finally sent to prison.

Life went back to normal, as normal as it could be. Before she got out, I had smoked some Sherm and had a Sherm attack. The cops were called on me, and I was taken to the crazy house. At first, I wouldn't get in the police car out of fear they would kill me. My mother had to get in first to get me in, and she had to ride all the way to the crazy house with me. I was admitted with no problem since I wasn't in my right mind. After seeing the doctor, they found they could do nothing with me, so I was hauled off to jail with no charges. I was put to sleep to calm my craziness, and after 24 hours of sleeping, I was released back to the streets, still feeling the Sherm. I walked from the jail to my mother's house, still high. When I got there, I zoned out and went completely crazy. I walked from her house to the Southside without saying a word to her. She didn't know what to think of me walking out without saying two words.

I jumped in a car with a friend, got paranoid, and rode to the next light. Then I jumped out of his car and ran, heading straight for the freeway. I crossed over eight lanes of speeding cars in both directions. Once across, I started thinking I was the only person left on the planet. I jumped a fence into a factory, approached a computer, and tried to find out what happened to the people on Earth. Seeing no answers, I ran and tried to steal a UPS truck. The cops were called on me again. They chased me off, and I jumped the fence and started walking down the street, still in a Sherm haze. As the police pulled up and said, "Freeze," I didn't understand. I ran behind the car for security. Something told me to jump in the police car and drive off, thinking he was telling me to take the car and go home. I tried to steal it, and the police officer tased me, shocking me until he got the cuffs on.

I hadn't been out an hour yet, and I was under arrest again. This time, I was charged with trying to steal a police vehicle and a UPS truck. My mind let the police know I wasn't in the right state. They placed me in a segregated cell, saying I was going crazy. The only difference was that this time, I knew I was going back to prison. When they came with a plea bargain for less time, I hurried up and signed. I was sent to prison a couple of days later. After only spending a month in the county, I was back in the yard where I ran into my family member who was finishing his ten-year sentence. In the yard together, he had all the drugs, even sacks of marijuana, which I smoked, calling it my escape.

In prison, where the weed was good, I stayed high. I guess you could say I used marijuana to cope with doing time. How else was I going to get through this without going crazy? Soon after arriving, I got a babysitter, which was my TV, thanks to my mother looking out for me. She would send me money during my time of need. Having a family member spend time with me made it easier. Here, where there was sunshine, unlike in the county jail where there was none, I did the rest of my time and got out, not knowing my next move would be a mistake.

Trying to get back with someone who didn't want to make it work was a problem I didn't need. Getting ready to get kicked out of her apartment, I got out with a little money and tried to bring her up to date on her rent, hoping I could stay with her instead of a halfway house. My parole officer wouldn't let me stay with her, so I had to go to a halfway house. Placing me there, I tried to make it work, but it was a place I had to pay to stay. Giving her my money, I didn't have money for them, so I was told I could only stay one night. Calling my parole officer the next day, he told me to come into his office for a visit. He told me since I couldn't afford a halfway house, I had to go to the homeless shelter. I didn't sign up for a homeless shelter and was called back into the parole office the next day. Going to see my parole officer, I didn't expect what was going to happen. He asked me to sit in the waiting room and secretly called the police on me, who quickly came and took me back to prison. I put up a fight, but they got me in cuffs. After being out for only ten days, I was back in prison.

I was processed and bound for Florence. After a seven-day stay at the processing center, I finally landed on the Florence North unit. I only had to do the time to kill my number, which was just two more months, and I would be free again. Serving my time in the army-like tents of the prison, I did the two months and was set free. Out now with a clean slate, no parole or probation, and no work history, I fell back into the drug trade, picking up a sack as soon as I got back to the streets. Things hadn't changed. The younger generation had all the corners, making selling crack harder. My little sack couldn't compare with the bigger sacks fools had, so I had to start fronting my dope to smokers, losing money with no turnaround in sight.

Now, being out for almost two months, I had to come up with another way to make money. I came up with the solution of buying a lot of weed. I thought the weed would help me win my girl back. Calling her up at work first, I got her to come over and help me bag it up. Bagging up a few hundred dollars' worth of weed, we sat at the homeboy's house and smoked, getting her to bite. We were now in the car making love. While undressing her, I couldn't take my eyes off her. Excited, I went in thinking I wasn't going to get any more. So, I beat up the Kitty cat, making both of us feel so good with ecstasy. As her body filled with so many emotions, she climbed on top of me and rode me like a stallion, causing my eyes to roll back in my head. By now, we were sweaty and filled with each other's fluids as we came into each other's arms. While I watched as Harmony filled the car, her panties now wet, she was ready to go.

But before she left, I asked her to take me to my brother's house to drop off some of the weed, taking a couple hundred dollars worth. We made it to my brother's house in no time, where we smoked out of my smoking bag and left an hour later. After heading back to the homeboy's house, she dropped me off. But before doing so, we sat in the car and talked for about an hour.

Just as we finished, a cop pulled up on us. Rolling down the window, the cop was hit with a gang of weed smoke in the face, causing him to want to pull us out of the car and search us and the car. I had over a pound of weed on me only because she made me go back in the house and get it before leaving for my brother's house. I wondered why I didn't leave it in my homeboy's house when I had the chance. But knowing it was her jealous ways that made me bring it made it my fault. She was searched first and found with two dime bags, two bags that I didn't know she tried to steal from me because I didn't even know she had them; when the cops found them, she knew she was busted. This made me realize she was still out for herself and ready to use me like she used everybody else.

Though trying to race back into the house as he handcuffed her, I did make it as the cop grabbed me and searched me. At first, missing the pound, he decided to search for me again, and this time, he found the pound. As he placed me in handcuffs, I knew I was going back to prison. This is when I realized dreams aren't for people like us. Here I was, dreaming about getting back with her, but I knew this weed charge would kill all that forever, with all hopes and promises being thrown out the door.

Getting stuck in jail that night, I was very stressed out. Now, being trapped in the county, I was praying and hoping for an OR release, thinking it was the only way for me to save my relationship with her. With every passing second, I was stressing out going through the process of jail, and I could see she was stressed out more than me sitting in a woman's holding tank. She wouldn't lay down and go to sleep. As it was her first time being locked up, I knew she didn't know what to expect. Her sitting on the edge of the bunk made me worry about her. I knew, no matter what, she would be getting out, it being her first time and all. The charges weren't too serious to hold her, so I told her not to worry. "You're going home on an OR, no matter what." Seeing the relief come over her, I went into the men's cell and went to sleep, waiting for the time to go to court.

Finally, the next day came, and we were taken in front of a judge who released us both on our own recognizance. A few hours later, she got out first. I told her to wait for me, which she did, as I was released a few minutes later. Greeting each other with a hug and a kiss, happy to be freed, we walked to the front of the jail and called her mother to come get us. Jumping in her mother's car, we rode to my homeboy's house and got her sister's car, where they dropped me off, leaving me with a lot to ponder. What's with the new case? And me heading to prison? Plus, what about the fact that she stole the weed from me? So, I didn't know if she loved me, but I definitely knew I couldn't trust her. Still being lost in love, I pursued her in hopes of trying to save this relationship before I went back to prison.

However, she disappeared for a couple of weeks, and I didn't get to see her. With no dollars and no way to come up, I guess I wasn't her type anymore. This became the turning point of our breakup as she showed her true colors. I guess she didn't want to see me unless I had money. I was just trying to collect every little dollar to get a little attention from her, which wasn't enough because she only came to pick up the money and leave, and I wouldn't see her again for another day or two. It didn't matter, though, because I thought I loved her. So, I didn't mind being gullible, thinking, is this what love was supposed to be like? I continued to let her use me, and as she went on to charge me for sex, I still didn't pull away until I went to prison.

I saw her two more times before I had to go back to court. The next time I saw her was at court, she wasn't there to give me support but to get judged for her own charges. Getting me to rally around her was easy. I was in love, after all. I was not worrying about my case because I was busy trying to comfort her. Given the postponement and leaving the court, I couldn't even leave with her as she was no longer studying me. Here, I was no longer on her mind, yet I was still in love with her. However, spending time with her was becoming a chore - a chore of me getting money just to have sex with her. That didn't matter to me as long as I could spend time with her.

By the time the next court date came, we were all but done. If we weren't done yet, the sentence I was about to receive was sure to end it. At court, where we both received our plea bargains, they came at her with a sweet deal. It was a deal of unsupervised probation and the promise to stay out of trouble for a year, meaning she didn't have to report to anybody, and she still could smoke her weed. But for me, things were different. I had more serious charges, and I knew I was facing some time in prison. Of my plea, they came with a three-year deal, and because I was not able to fight this in trial, I signed the plea. After all, I was caught red-handed. I was thinking that if she had never gotten jealous and made me bring the weed with me, I wouldn't have this case now. But given 30 more days of freedom before sentencing, we left the courtroom together, and I knew it was over.

Feeling the distance wash over us, I could see she was pushing away. Now teetering on the brink of depression, I was sad all the time as I was missing her. I knew I would be going to prison, but that didn't help. By now, full-blown depression had set in. Before my upcoming court date, I was in and out of the crazy house. No matter what, I was still determined to get her back, which was only me fighting a lost cause.

Now, 30 days later, I was back in court, but not too much had happened as I was given another 30-day postponement. So, I took my depression to the danger zone and started hanging out with family. I couldn't get much done because I was too depressed, as seeing her had become a thing of the past. She became the reason Love doesn't live here anymore.

Staying out any longer was getting harder, so I started trying to hang around her again. While we fought all the time over some stupid stuff, realizing her heart wasn't the place for me, I did everything in my power to try and make it a place for me.

I remembered one day how I needed $1.25 to get to my mother's job in order to earn some money, with the amount reserved for the bus fare. As I was clearly on the other side of town from my mother's job, and the bus was the fastest way to get there, I tried to get it out of her, but she wouldn't give it to me. Having enough of the arguing, I got up and walked out of her house feeling very mad. I was so mad that I busted her two front windows on my way out. She quickly ran and called the police.

I left before they got there so they couldn't apprehend me. By the time they arrived, I was already on the bus, headed for my mother's job. Reaching her job, I got the $100 and headed back to the townhouse, where I was dodging to stay away from her house. Knowing she would call the police again, I tried to dodge her as much as I could. So, I went to my aunt's house, where she got word that I was there and did exactly as I said she would do; she called the police again.

Not wanting them to come to my auntie's house, I ran and hid at my cousin's house. Having seen her entering my cousin's house, she directed the police to the house. By now, everybody had run in and barricaded themselves in the house, leaving the police to bang on the door, wanting to get in. But no one would open the door for them until all the banging and beating started getting to my cousin, who was thinking that the police were gonna break down her door. So, she opened it and let them in.

Before they could enter, I had run into the bathroom and locked myself in, bracing myself between the bathroom sink and the door so they couldn't get in. I could hear them clearing out the house and getting ready to get me. So when they came, they negotiated with me for about an hour before I came out of the bathroom. They handcuffed me and took me to the jail, taking me outside. I had seen they had yellow-taped the apartment off. I didn't notice the severity of the police being there, but once at the station, I was charged with two felony counts. I was out on another felony count, so I knew I wasn't going anywhere, as I was held without bond when I went to see the judge, only to be housed here in the county jail on the second floor.

A month later, I was sitting back before the judge. This time, I ran into two of my homeboys from the South side, who had to see the same judge. Finally, we were led into the judge's chambers, where, one by one, we went before the judge, who didn't release anybody. Sitting there, waiting for my turn to go before the judge, I never went before the judge, as it was getting late and the judge had to leave. Finally, good news came from the courtroom. My lawyer came and told me I wouldn't be seeing the judge and that I would be released today.

I was taken back to the holding cells, where I would wait to get transferred to the second floor in preparation for my release. Thinking it should take no longer than two hours for me to get out, I sat there and watched TV. Two hours went by, and I still hadn't been released yet; then, five hours went by, and it was time for a lockdown. I still hadn't been released yet, so I lay down and went to sleep, just to be woken up around two o'clock in the morning for my release. Waking up, I was told to roll up. So I gathered up all my stuff and headed downstairs. Taken to the release cell, I was given my clothes and dressed out. About 30 minutes later, I was led out the door to freedom.

Once out, I walked to my mother's house, and she gave me a ride back to the townhouses. I wanted to rub it in her face that I was out. As she wondered how it was out, my days were still numbered. Having about two months left for freedom, I was still being sent to prison. After putting up with her for two months, finally, the court came, and they had my plea bargain all set up. They wanted me to take a year for busting her windows and two years for the marijuana. I signed the plea bargain. The only good thing about this plea bargain was that probation was available.

Given my last 30 days of freedom before sentencing, I decided to use these 30 days to try and talk my way into getting probation. Contemplating all month long about what I would say to the judge; all kinds of thoughts went through my head, but I couldn't come up with one way or the other on how to get probation. I just prayed it would come to me when I went back to court. Thinking it was my last 30 days of freedom, I sat back and got high every day of the 30 days before I had to go to court. Getting so high I didn't know if I was coming or going.

Finally, the 30 days came and went, and it was time to go back to court. Waking up, I smoked two blunts and dressed while I was waiting. Then I caught the bus to my mother's house, who was already up and prepared to take me to court. Arriving at the court building, we went up to the floor where the courtroom was. Sitting there, my attorney hadn't arrived yet. Finally, some 20 minutes later, he walked into the courtroom, and some 15 minutes later, I was in front of the judge. Reading my charges and telling me what he was going to do, the judge asked me if I had any last words to say before sentencing. Scared and frightened, I mustered up every word in my body to ask for probation. It worked because the judge turned around and gave me intensive probation and didn't sentence me to prison.

Leaving the courtroom, happiness washed over my body like a river. I was told to go home and wait for my probation officer to come by. What did I do? I went to her house and started smoking weed. Knowing I was supposed to go straight home and wait for my probation officer, I did the opposite. At her house, I didn't care about the probation because all I was thinking about was trying to get into her pants. Talking her into letting me spend the night, we ended up buying some Hennessy, which we drank and made love all night long. Finishing finally, we went to sleep.

Waking up happy, I was taken home, where I had to wait for my probation officer. When he finally came to see me, he told me about all the rules and regulations of probation. Living at my mother's house,

I was on probation and couldn't go anywhere. When my mother went to look for me in the apartment, she went by herself. I knew staying with her would be short-lived because her husband did not want me there. I was glad that day that she found me an apartment I could move into without the permission of my probation officer. He didn't come by that day, so I had to wait until the next day to get his permission to move into my apartment. After all the arguments with her husband, I couldn't wait to get out of his apartment.

Finally, the next day, my probation officer came through and gave me permission to move. Packing up, I took a bunch of pillows and covers to make a pallet on the floor. Now that I had my own place, no one could tell me anything. But I stayed home for the probation, at least for now. Falling asleep, I was awakened by a knock at the door. I answered it, and it was my surveillance officer. For the first time, she was introducing herself to me, telling me to be home because she would be by at all hours of the day and night.

The next time I saw her was at three in the morning when she asked me to blow into a breathalyzer to see if I had been drinking. I hadn't, and I blew all zeroes. Leaving, she told me she'd be by in a couple of hours. So I sat and waited for her, like I did on a daily basis. The next day came, and she was taking too long to come by. Finally showing up, we did our thing, and she left again. As soon as she left, my friend and his girlfriend showed up, saying they had been kicked out by his mother. I said they could stay with me. When my surveillance officer came back, she saw I had company. Quickly asking them their names, she gave me a breathalyzer and left.

Beforehand, she told me she was going to run their names for warrants. He said he was clean, and she said she had a warrant for running away. She started worrying about my surveillance officer, asking questions like, was I going to jail? I told her not to worry about it because she wouldn't run her name. I finally got her to calm down, and we decided to go to my brother's house. Knowing I wasn't supposed to because I was on house arrest, I went anyway with no intentions of drinking or getting high until I saw weed and drink. As temptation set in, I drank and smoked, but not to excess. Thinking maybe this wouldn't get me in trouble. By the time we left, you couldn't tell if I had been drinking or smoking.

Heading back to my house, I saw my surveillance officer had come by. I knew I was in trouble. She left a note saying I better be home when she came back. I sat there and waited for the drink and marijuana to wear off. The weed was good, but the breathalyzer still showed that I had been drinking. This being my last straw, she ordered me to her office the next day. Falling asleep all that night, I prayed they wouldn't lock me up. But finding out the next day that my prayers fell on deaf ears. Once I reached the probation office, I was asked to come into this back office, where I had to talk to my probation officer supervisor. Telling them my life story didn't help because some 15 or 20 minutes later, I was in handcuffs and on my way to the county jail again, this time for a probation violation.

Resisting the urge to fight and go off, I just let them take me to jail, thinking I didn't need any more charges. In hopes that I might get out again, I went through the night court process, where I was told what I already knew: that probation violation was non-bondable. I was sent to Max holding, where they put me on the 2nd floor, and I was made to wait until my next court date. Time went fast, and it was time for my next court date already.

While sitting in jail, I decided to take the 2 1/2 years in prison instead of getting reinstated on intensive probation, all because I knew

I couldn't do probation in the first place. Getting sentenced the same day I signed the plea bargain; I didn't have long to wait in the county jail. I would be joining my sister, who had just been sentenced to 6 1/2 years in prison, along with our brother, who was serving a 5-year sentence for narcotics possession and sales. A week after my sentencing, they sent me to the Towers jail, where I had to wait in the Department of Corrections pod to be sent to the Department of Corrections. Two weeks after that, I was sent to DOC. Leaving intake, I was sent to Lewis prison, where I settled in to do my time.

Hitting Lewis, everybody was in the yard. Some friends and a few family members showed me love, giving me this and that to start out with. Like always, I got a care package when I came. The yard was up and running already, with certain people having drugs and certain people having drinks. It was like we were at home. As I got my portion of that pill, I started to move around the yard to see what I could get my hands into. Nobody wanted to be here, but we were here. Running around the yard, I ran into a few blood cats who knew me from the streets. Knowing I was more of a leader type, they made me the leader of the Bloods. Now, I had my own crew. Holding it down for the Bloods and getting our portion of the drug trade was priority number one. Never one to extort the weak, we also had to protect those we thought didn't have any say. The prison was more political than ever now, as it was a place where politics took the forefront and where every race wanted to be in charge. Mostly, it was a place where they didn't leave you alone, where men preyed on men.

With the strong surviving, I went on about doing my time without any problems from anyone. My reputation exceeded itself; I was known as one not to mess with. Now doing the most, I was right in the middle of things, smack dab in the thick of it. But it didn't bother me as long as the police didn't get wind of what I was doing. Here is where my time took a turn for the worse. I started worrying about what I no longer had, and that was her. Opening up, I started dreaming about her every night and thinking about her all day. My every waking thought was about her, and all she kept doing was ignoring me. Still doing my thing; nothing could take my mind off her. So I walked around and thought of her. There were days when I thought she was right there with me. I would be rudely awakened by the sound of them unlocking doors just to know the reality of being in prison.

So I sat down to write her. I poured my heart out in every letter, praying that I could reach her through my writing. I wrote every chance I got, writing at least one letter a day for 30 days straight. Getting no response, my writing trailed off for a little while, going to every other day, then to every week. I just said to forget it, but I will write once a month. Not once did she write back. Thinking if she just wrote one letter, it would make my year, and that's all I would need: one letter. Boy, how she hurt and disappointed me when she didn't write back. When that one letter never came, I stopped writing her altogether. But in my heart, I didn't give up on her.

I started thinking about whether she had forgotten about me. With all the time we spent together in a relationship, how could she forget about me? Telling myself she must have; I still couldn't let her go. Doing time without her made doing time that much harder. Thinking how could I stop loving her when I can't even stop thinking about her? Telling myself she's my all started to set in. I worked on how I could get her back when I got out. Knowing I would love her always, no matter what, I told myself I had to get over her. But how could I get over her when I can't stop loving her?

Now that time was moving on, and I still hadn't heard from her, I started to think the worst. Was she out there hurt? Did somebody do something to her? Did she let someone steal her heart? A year went by, and I still hadn't heard from her. Then I lost her address. Only then did I stop writing. But I still thought of her, sometimes even shedding a tear. Telling myself I should man up, I brought myself to the point where I vowed never to love again. I vowed to give no other woman a chance to break my heart again. Though the world didn't know, I wanted the world to know that she was the last woman I would ever love. Even though I needed her at this moment of time, I had to figure out how to make myself strong without her. So that's what I did. I sat down and concentrated on myself.

Chapter Thirteen:
Love, Loss, And Redemption

Six months earlier, I was taken to reclass, and my score dropped from a 3-3 to a 3-2. After everything, there I was again a year later, and I was reclassed again. This time, my score went from a 3-2 to a 2-1. I thought to myself that now I could be sent from this medium yard to a minimum yard, where I would have more freedom, where I could run the yard and do my thing at the same time. By now, everybody was leaving for minimum yards, and now it was my turn. I was officially breaking up the crew by leaving.

However, I knew it would not be before the crystal meth and heroin had hit, along with the weed. We mostly smoked up, selling the heroin and meth to the white boys and Mexicans or whoever wanted to buy it. We sold very small amounts of marijuana because we needed it to get high, mainly using it for our escape. It was an escape without escaping, you could call it. Smoking every chance we got kept us wanting more. So we just smoked until it was all gone, just to wait for it to hit again, which was usually every week.

Most of the time, we would do it all without any questions asked. We simply loved it when it was time to escape. I tried to be a part of every smoke session there was, bringing in new homeboys that I met during my time in prison - people who were serving time all over the state, from little towns that I would meet and plan to visit once I was out.

The few times I went to see them, we would talk about how I used to go there and serve. But mostly, I would learn something new about that town from them every time they talked. At that point, I couldn't help but think that if life was a game that money could buy, then the rich folks would live and the poor would die. Just knowing life is hard against all odds, I tried to carry on.

Around this time, while still in the penitentiary, one of my girls' mother had passed away. She was feeling negative about the world as she wrote to me and told me, sending me an obituary. I tried to comfort her with the letter I wrote back. When I didn't hear back from her, I didn't know how to ease her pain, so I didn't know how to comfort her after that. In the yard with one of her family members, I told him his aunt had passed. He had no idea about the news, but he was glad I told him. More and more homeboys that I knew from the street started coming in. I didn't know that one of the homeboys I grew up with was in the yard, who was finishing up a 15.75-year sentence. After getting to kick it with him for six months, my time on the maximum yard was over. I was told to roll up my gear because I was leaving the yard. I packed it up and sat everything by the door for inventory. Given an orange jumpsuit that I had to put on, along with my flip-flops, it was the only way that I could travel. The next day, I was on my way, Florence North unit bound.

Not knowing what to expect, I rode the bus in silence, finally arriving a couple of hours later. I am now settled into my new home, as intake went quickly. During the long, quiet ride, all I could do was think of her on the bus. Lost in my thoughts, I wondered who was holding her at this early hour of the morning. I got heartbroken and wanted to cry, but I held it in as the love of my life was still on my mind. Even thinking about what I could possibly do without her in my life, I knew then and there that I wanted her back. I couldn't help but wonder: *is it wrong to love someone so much who didn't know I was even alive?* But it was nothing because now I'm what they called a dogged-out OG.

I decided that as soon as I hit the streets, I was going to get back on my feet, and my mind was going to be on nothing but money. However, being placed in the army-like tent jail of the prison where we didn't have free range to go into any tent or roam yards one and three, I was stuck in yard two. Somehow, we made it work, getting what we needed to the yards and getting what we needed from the other yards. The lockdown came, and now it was nightfall, so I lay down and went to sleep, spending my first night in the Florence North unit.

Onto my property, they finally called me to come get my property, give me a pass to go to yard one, and pick it up. Finally, I had my babysitter and my TV. Setting up all my stuff in my space, I sat down and watched TV for a little while, then got up and got into the swing of things. Finding out who had what and who was bringing in what was easy, so I put my two cents in and came out with a lot, becoming one of the main men in no time at all. I ran into a number of Bloods - some from Phoenix and some from Tucson. There, I met only a few crabs that became my friends, and we formed a new crew of not-to-be-messed-with gang, where everybody was his own man.

When the money started coming in for me, I was into the groove of things being the man, so I made this my new home away from home. By now, for some reason, time started speeding up, and it seemed like my time was going by faster. This is when the talk about moving prisoners from this state to other states outside of Arizona began. Being one who wanted to go, I got no luck and had to stay in Arizona, stuck here in these army-like tents. Everybody started rolling up for yard one and yard two, even people coming in after me and the ones that got to leave before me, even though I was there first. It started bothering me that they would leave first, but I shook it off and said it would be my turn one day. Then, I would be out of the tents and into a warm dorm. For now, I just stayed where I was. Finally, after spending four months in the tents, I was moved to yard two, where I had the comfort of being inside.

While in prison, one of my homegirls started having problems with her boyfriend. I got a letter from her letting me know that her boyfriend had shot her in the head, not killing her but wounding her badly. She survived and went on with her life while he went to jail. A few weeks went by, and my ex, the one I considered myself in love with, though she wasn't mine anymore, wrote me and told me that her boyfriend had shot her too. I wondered how stupid she could be to get with somebody that would hurt her. I thought she wasn't a G anymore because after he shot her, she ended up staying with him anyway.

I knew this couldn't be what we'd come to. I guessed that if love had ever been a factor, then she would've been there by my side, but she wasn't. So, there I sat, broken-hearted. It hurt knowing my girls weren't my girls anymore. During this time, I would be doing it by myself from here on out. It was the first time that I was truly alone.

As I had already come of age, I was no longer a slave to either woman. Walking the rest of the way with my head held high, I did the rest of my time with ease, having no girls to worry about. It had me growing all the time now. Gone were the days of old. I vowed to live on the right side of the law when I got out this time.

This mindset didn't last long. I heard about one of my homeboys being shot up, and it had me kind of worried for him. As I knew at the time that I couldn't lose another homeboy, when word got back that he would survive, I started feeling better about myself. I was only mad that I couldn't be there to retaliate with him against whoever shot him.

This made me think about the two homeboys that I had already lost. Reminiscing about the days when they were alive would often put a smile on my face. I did not forget about the Eastside homeboy. Rest in peace, my dogs.

I was not signing up for this no-letter stuff. As I was getting no letters any longer, I started looking at everybody differently; those who forgot about me, I forgot about them. After two years and some change, the top of the year had turned, and I only had about six months to go. The remainder of my time went by fast. Having no problems, I got out about six months later. I was free and back to the world.

I was happy, though I went looking for both my girls, just to see what kind of chance I would have with either of them in love. The only chance I got was when I got to sleep with both of them one more time, not at the same time, but on different occasions.

I made love to her, then turned around and made love to the other one. With the first one, it was just as amazing as it was with the other. With her, as I went down on her, I didn't stop until she came all over my face. All hot and bothered, she begged me to put it in. Obliging her, I must have worked for about two hours. The more I went in and out, the wetter she got. And with me trying to dry it out, I kept pumping, thinking this was exactly what I needed from her. Even though making love to her put me where I wanted to be, I made love to her all night without falling asleep, knowing this would be my last time. Then I got up, got dressed, and left. After all, she did get rid of her man for a night of making love to me. A few days went by, and I was now inside her. We sweated up the sheets through making love, and eating her out had her creaming all over me—another night of not wanting to stop for fear of never getting it again. We took a shower, did it again, and then I had to go. As they both left me not knowing if I was coming or going, it had me lost for a few days.

This is when I stepped into my mind and lost all grip on reality, to the point where I was roaming the streets, talking to myself. Going out of my mind, I tried to play stick-up kid and started robbing stores. One day, lost in thought, I tried to rob a store and ended up getting caught. Dreaming no more, I found myself back in jail three months after I had just gotten out of prison. Only this time, with more serious charges—charges where I would face serious time. Sitting in the county for about six months, I finally got sentenced to 9 1/2 years. A week later, I was back in the prison yard, this time for the long haul. I felt like I never left; I just settled right back in. Only this time, I brought with me that "I don't care" attitude.

I was only in prison for a week when I started to rebel against everything and got put on "pay him no mind" status because they thought I was crazy. Joining her little brother, my little brother, who was doing natural life for a murder he didn't commit, I started reminiscing about him in the days of old. I remembered how I tried to get him to run on the murder beef, where I tried to get him to go out of town with me. But insisting he was innocent and could beat the murder, he decided to stay and fight after he got caught. Now doing natural life, over the last 25 years, my little brother has become strong and is now a force to be reckoned with in the penitentiary. During our time on different yards, I used to hear about the things he got into. Plus, I heard about how he beat up the guard and went to lockdown for about three or four years. Communicating here and there, we did our time and got left alone, which is how we would have it—no other way.

But here in prison, in the yard I was on, they finally came to me and told me I wouldn't be going to a minimum yard. I would have to remain on a medium yard for the remainder of my time, all because I was gang-affiliated and had the tattoos to prove it. So, already, I had strikes against me. Here it was, now six months into doing my time. My insanity caused me to get into a fight, losing it as I beat up this crab from some West Side hood, paranoid, thinking he had my name in his mouth. This was only the first of many fights to come. Though my mind wouldn't let me comprehend that I was doing time, it wouldn't let me give up on myself either, telling me to fight, which is why I fought. Then I started to fight through the madness as it became me versus my mind. Knowing I needed help, here is where I started to get help from them in the fight against my mind. Or should I say, here is where they joined the fight between them, me, and my mind?

Placing me on meds, I went from insanity to sanity in no time at all. Still, my mind wouldn't let me comprehend that I was doing time, so I did it under the pretense that I was free. Then one month turned to two, and two months turned to three, and the next thing you knew,

I had three months left. Here's where I started to have one foot out the door with the other foot in prison, and you couldn't tell me I wasn't free yet. Now that I was so close to freedom, I was taking more and more chances of staying locked up. Being careful, I got around the police, though. With two of the three months I had left breezing by, it started to settle in that I had one month left, which seemed to drag on as the slowest days of my life. But I was determined to finish this time and get out.

Dragging now, I was down to a week left in prison after three weeks had passed by. Now, time was really dragging as I started to count the seconds of the day, unable to sleep because I was anxious that I was getting out. I stayed up most of the nights, sleeping here and there for an hour or two at a time. Then, three days passed by, leaving me with four to go, and these were the four slowest days of my life. And the next thing you knew, I was free. But that was then. This is now.

As I sat on a fresh 9 1/2-year sentence to go, I thought, *how could God bring me back to this miserable place to do this miserable time?* I found myself thinking maybe it was time for me to die because I made a deal with God that if I were to die soon, he would send me to jail instead. So, I could look at the situation from the perspective of Him saving my life. With more to do in life, I just sat back and did my time, having family and friends come through on their way in and out. It made my time go by a little easier and faster. The first three to five years went by so fast that I didn't realize I had just done five years. With the last three years slowing down to a medium pace, I just went with the flow.

By now, the spice was plentiful in the penitentiary, and it had me smoking it because weed was scarce and hard to find, coming in on an every now and then humbug. Don't get me wrong, when it came in, I got my hands on it, and I smoked it, not caring about a dirty UA. But with no way to detect spice, everybody was smoking it. Smoking it excessively had me going off my meds, and I started to retreat back into insanity.

As I started flipping out, doctors at the prison thought I should have my brain examined. So, they took me from the prison to a hospital in Tucson and gave me a brain scan. They stuck me in this machine that freaked me out. Stuck, all kinds of paranoia went through my mind. Seeing that I was freaking out, they took me out of the machine, told me to calm down, and let me rest for a little while. Calming down, I finished the brain scan and was taken back to the prison.

I told myself at least I got a trip out of prison to see the beautiful nurses and women walking through the hospital. Getting my head right, they kept me there day and night until they could figure out the right meds to put me on. Whatever concoction they gave me worked because it became a temporary fix for my madness and made me sane again.

I picked up where I left off with the spice smoke, but this time, I didn't go off my meds. Now that my brain was at ease, I could cope with the time I was doing, even with the outside world going on without me. Being stuck in the penitentiary didn't bother me anymore. I settled in to finish my time and calmed down. Though time went on and everybody grew, I separated myself from the streets. Still dreaming dreams? I learned the hard way that dreams aren't for people like us. Up to this point, none of my dreams had come true—not even the dream of freedom, which I dreamed every night.

But time went on, and here I was, eight years later, finally freed. Things had changed on this side; it was like I was on an alien planet. The game was no longer for me. I didn't know what I was going to do to make money, so I went with the flow and started roaming the streets. Homeless now, with no resources to get my meds, my mind started playing tricks on me again. I needed help more than anybody, but I couldn't find any. For months, I walked around going crazy, spiraling further as time went on until one day, the cops picked me up and took me to the crazy house.

It took three or four months to get me back in my right mind and somewhat sane. When they released me back to the streets, I was more on the sane side, enough to cope with the streets, though not quite like other people. Even though I was coming around, nobody needed to be in their right mind more than me, or I wouldn't survive in this world where madness was driving me mad. I was afraid to pick up a gun because of what I might do to others and to myself, so I stayed away from them this time around. With everybody packing, I was already in harm's way, and being crazy only put me further at risk. Not knowing what I was doing, I would run up on anybody, gun or no gun in hand. I was crazy—who would stop from shooting me?

After I had been released from the crazy house and returned to the streets, I focused on my money this time, aiming to do something legal or at least something with a lesser risk of doing time. I came up with the idea of getting my Social Security back since I was out of my mind and deserved my crazy check. So I went to the Social Security Office and came out with my check. Thinking I now had an income, I could focus on finding a place to stay. I realized quickly that my Social Security check wouldn't cover the rent of an apartment, so I had to come up with another way to get more money. I checked into a mental health clinic for outpatient help, where they had me sign up for a housing voucher for low-income housing. But the waiting list was two to three years long.

Still homeless, I decided to keep roaming the streets, sleeping in parks and on bus stops. After doing this for a year and then some, I ended up losing my meds just as another episode was around the corner. Losing it, I ended up back in the crazy house, where it took two months to get me right again. On my release date, I told them I was homeless. They told me they couldn't release me homeless, which made me think they were going to keep me in the crazy house permanently. I started to panic, but they told me to calm down and that they had something better in store for me.

As I anxiously waited for them to return, they came back with vouchers for low-income housing. Still on the waiting list at my mental health clinic, but now I didn't have to wait. With a voucher in hand, I was released and went on a hunt for an apartment. At first, it was hard to find one because of my felony record. My voucher was set to expire in three or four months, and at the two-month mark, after not finding an apartment, I asked my mental health clinic for a navigator—someone who finds apartments for you. But I didn't receive a navigator until the three-month mark of my voucher expiration, leaving me with one month to go. Luckily, a week later, she found me an apartment in a place run by a slumlord. Being a felon, I had to take what I could get, so I moved in the next day.

Upon moving in, I saw smokers and dope dealers running around the apartments. At first, I didn't want to bring that to my doorstep. I sat back for a year, observing the smokers and drug dealers' every routine until I got it down pat. Not wanting to pick up a crack sack, I decided to sell weed instead, which brought customers to my doorstep. It wasn't fast money like selling crack, but it was just as profitable, with less foot traffic coming to the door. As the money came, I started stacking again and could now afford to pay my bills. I even made enough money to buy a car—a decommissioned police cruiser, a Tahoe. It took a year, but I fixed it up with new rims and music, giving it the best red paint job I could.

Now, I called myself living, and I didn't want it to stop. But around my third year of making money, things started to take a turn for the worse. Somehow, I went off my meds again, flipping out for days until I got arrested for petty theft. After spending a week in jail, I was released, still out of my mind. I returned home, walking around the house and talking to myself until there was a knock at the door. A friend had come by, telling me he was hungry, so I turned on the stove to cook something. Deciding to cook chicken, we put a pot of grease on the stove with the intention of frying it, but we forgot the grease was on the stove. After leaving it for too long, it turned into a grease fire, burning down my kitchen.

I was displaced from my apartment for a week while they started repairs. A week later, after the repairs were done, I was called into the office and told I had to move. They were kicking me out of the apartment, citing that I had put other residents in danger with the fire. Thinking I was going to lose my voucher, I begged them not to kick me out, but it fell on deaf ears, and I was forced to go. So, I manned up and left. Given two days to get out, I packed my stuff the next day and moved. I went straight to the housing office and explained my situation, and they saw it wasn't my fault and gave me another voucher. I took it and went looking for another apartment. This time, I didn't wait too long to get a navigator, who found me an apartment in no time.

This time, I found a way better apartment that wasn't under any slumlords. There weren't any smokers or drug dealers walking around here, so I knew my weed-selling business would be put out of business. But having Social Security and a voucher kept a roof over my head. Though it left me with no extra money to do anything, where there's a will, there's a way. I let a new hustle fall into my lap—one that would keep me out of jail, put extra money in my pocket, and had a low risk of getting caught. Taking it in stride, I just collected the extra money, and with it continuing to come in, I wasn't willing to let it go.

Around this time, a lot of the homeboys who had finished serving their time were getting released, along with some family members who I knew were happy to get out. Remembering here is where she tried to come back into my life and play me, which I didn't mind because I told myself I would always love her. She was the first, the only, and the last love of my life. We started out with me having to get her drunk and high to make love to her, which I didn't mind because I drank and smoked, too. Plus, I really wanted to be with her.

So I called her up and told her I had some Hennessy and some weed, and asked if she could come over. She told me yeah, and hurried up and rushed over. Wanting to see her naked, I had her undress and walk around in front of me in the nude. I couldn't believe how lucky I was. Watching her luscious body got me a hard-on, almost making me rush into having sex with her. We sat back, smoked, and drank. She sat in the chair, opening and closing her legs to tease me with what she had between them. We got pretty wasted, drinking half the Hennessy and smoking half the weed, which got her hot and bothered.

I moved closer and started sucking on her chest, sticking my finger between her legs, and I could see how wet she was. I got on the ground on my knees and started eating her out. With every twist of my tongue, she was summoning. Unable to take it anymore, she told me to climb inside her. Putting her legs on my shoulders, I took her right there in the chair, keeping her in that position for 30 minutes. Soaking up the chair, we decided to move to the bed. I ravished her until we could take it no more. With both of us climaxing at the same time, we collapsed.

We lay there, filled with each other's fluids. I fell asleep with my hand still between her legs. I woke up an hour later with my hand still there while she slept. I watched her for another 30 minutes until she woke up. We decided to drink and smoke the rest of the alcohol and weed. Still naked, we started getting horny again but didn't make love again until we finished the alcohol and weed. This time, it was even better than the first. Then she had to go home to her boyfriend, who probably made love to her too. But that wasn't my problem; she wasn't my girl, so it didn't bother me.

She returned the next day so we could do it all over again, which ended up with us doing it all that week. Then, I guess she got tired of me because she stopped coming around for a while. This is what started her coming around only when she needed money, where she would exchange it for sex. I started asking myself how many friends she had and if she was doing this with them too. The thought of her having too many led me to stop giving her money. I told her I only had weed and drink for her sex, which, on most occasions, she was okay with. Until we fell out over me not giving her money, and we stopped speaking. This is when I told myself I would train myself to get over her, and not seeing her for a year helped. Although I still somewhat have feelings for her, I now know I could go on without her.

When the year was up, I got another chance to see her. Going through the same game-playing, I told her I was done with her tricks - that I wasn't going to give her any money. But I would get her drunk and high if she made love to me. She got mad and stormed out, trying to take the drink and weed with her. Not having that, she knew what she had to do, so she came back in, and we got drunk, high, and made love all night. Then, and only then, did I let her go home to her boyfriend, wondering if it would be the last time I saw her. But it wasn't the last time, because I got her to come over and christen my new apartment.

Here is where I really made love to her and tried to kill her guts, wanting to make love to her to try and get her to stay, which was to no avail. I guess I didn't beat it up good enough. So when she gave me some more for a second time, I tried to make love to her in a passionate way, but that didn't get her to stay either. I told myself I must've scared her off because I hadn't seen her for a while after that. Even though she knew where I stayed, she still didn't come by. I told myself to forget her and just move on. Though I don't sit around missing her, I still think about her. But that's just me. Hoping it wasn't, but if it is goodbye, then goodbye to my first, only, and last love.

Now, with her, it was a different story. Vowing to never make love to me again, she never made love to me again ever since. As I recall the last time we made love, I now realize it's been a long time. I do miss her and might still be in love with her, but she doesn't know it. It's hard to tell someone like her that you still love her. I never told her and just became her best friend. We've been close friends ever since. Maybe one day, I'll get the courage to tell her that I still love her, hoping she believes and trusts me enough to get her to come back home.

Here's my message to her: *I dream of you coming back to me often, and it hurts because I didn't know if you'd be coming back or not. But it was when I dreamed about getting between your legs and getting some of that big red snapper that killed me.* It has been so long since I last

170

touched her, or been near her, or been inside her. I only have memories of what she felt like and looked like. I ask myself, *does your pearl tongue still stick out? Those of us who had you only know how it is. I also want to know if it's still good and tight, or did you mess it up with all the new friends and your boyfriend? I know you like having her played with because I never saw you alone. Even though you look lonely, like there's something missing in your life, the way you like playing the field shows me you're not ready to settle down. So I sit back and wait for you to get all of that out of your system. Know that I'm here for you if you want someone to love you - someone who won't cheat on you, someone who will give you his honest opinion, and someone who will love you forever. I will be here waiting for you forever.*

Around this time, my life fell into hardship with the sudden death of two of my baby mothers. First, she died of some kind of organ failure after going through dialysis for years. They finally found her an organ and gave her a transplant, but it didn't take. Now, my son and daughter's mother is gone. Preceding her in death was our daughter, who died in a car accident a year or so before her mother. Now I can't believe I'm missing them both. *Rest in peace, most beautiful women. Know that you are loved and missed.*

Then, a few months later, my other baby mother succumbed to death. She had a medical problem, but nobody knew what it was, and it finally killed her. As I was on good terms with her, I went to see her being put to rest, where I saw my son for the first time in 18 years. Meeting him, I got the hug of a lifetime, and I was incredibly happy to see him - so happy that I didn't want to pull away.

While going into the church, I walked past her casket and said my proper goodbyes. Simply saying that I missed her would have been an understatement. Leaving, I relished the chance of seeing my son, who

I hoped knew that his mother was in a better place. My message to her is: *Rest in peace, and know that you are missed and loved.*

Now, I didn't know my fifth baby mama would shock me. I never expected what she did next. After getting slapped by some dude she knew, she took her car and ran him over for revenge just to get arrested and sent to prison. The one person who I thought would never go to prison was now in prison. Writing her, I found out she didn't want to have anything to do with me, which was okay because I didn't want to have anything to do with her. Even though, at one point, she loved me, I was just using her for sex. I knew she was somewhat mad at me for getting her pregnant after I got her sister pregnant, and for that, she couldn't stand me. It wasn't my fault she opened her legs as we kept making love behind her sister's back. As I had been with her sister first, how could I have known that she'd be willing to share herself with me? This resulted in me having a baby by two sisters, with her love dying for me as a result. However, she didn't stop loving her sister. I guess I couldn't take away family love even by putting babies in both of them.

Finally, with both sisters turning their backs on me, I finally got her to forgive me before her passing, which put me at ease. All I had to do was get the other sister to forgive me. I just wanted her to get over the fact that we have a son together, or at least not view it so negatively. Now, I just hope she knows it's not the end of the world. Bringing something so joyous and beautiful into the world shouldn't make her hate me.

However, as for dreaming a dream that wasn't for me, I had to move on. I no longer wanted to be a part of the criminal life. I don't ever want to go back to prison. Now, I see that living on the right side of the law has me headed in the right direction. Feeling lonely at the top made me feel alienated. Though girls came and went, I still couldn't find that special someone for me, so this caused me to go celibate for a while. With no woman in my life, I was able to keep up with my bills instead of spending my money on them, which is what I used to do to try and impress them. After all this time, I now have no woman around. It has enabled me to get ahead of the things in my life, and I like being ahead. Looking ahead, I look forward to meeting her - the one I'm supposed to love. I set out on my quest in search of her. Though she eludes me, I know she's out there, so I won't give up on looking for her. Sometimes, I feel like I'm dreaming a lost dream as she still hasn't crossed my path. Though I feel like I'm losing hope, I try to hold on to it, but constantly wondering where she's at has started to wear on me.

I just want to say to her, "Wherever you are, I promise to keep walking the path that's headed in your direction if you keep walking in the path that heads in my direction. Maybe one day we will finally meet. And now I look forward to that day. Then, we will let no man come between what God has brought together."

Chapter Fourteen:
The Illusion Of Dreams

Now that I've begun to understand life a little, I could bring myself to cope with the world. But veering back into reality, I realized that I had been out of the game for about 20 years, and yet I still continued to make mediocre money. I noticed that whatever little money I had was going towards bills. As it would take another year or two, I decided to jump back into the game. Picking up a sack was new to me, and I decided I wouldn't sell rocks again. Instead, I went for selling halves and wholes because I thought selling rocks would be too slow for me. Starting out slow, it seemed like I would never make any money, as the customers just weren't coming. But that didn't discourage me because with the product I had, I knew it would go sooner or later, even though it was later than sooner. I just sat on the product, and since I wasn't in a rush to lose money, I would sit on it forever if I had to.

Bringing in my little brother, we decided to make a go of the game again and get as much money as we could. This time, determined to get a house, I knuckled down, remembering the spot—the one with two weeks left before we got kicked out. We set in motion to get as much money as we could out of it before then. I told myself that this had to work because I was tired—tired of being a have-not. I thought something had to give, not wanting to live like this anymore. Plus, for one dream, any dream, to come true, I strayed away from the idea that dreams aren't for people like me. Even if only for a second, I still hoped. I was so tired of being at the bottom that I stopped caring that it was lonely at the top, which is where I was trying to make it. And as far away as it was, I still saw light at the end of the tunnel—or so I thought. It was light, but how could I know what I was looking at? So, as I looked further, I decided I would find my way, even without knowing where I was going. Not one to believe in luck, I didn't think I would get lucky, but I told myself I didn't have time to worry about that anyway.

Around this time, I was sitting at home watching TV when the news came on. I saw the most shocking news I could see—a picture of him as a wanted man, wanted for first-degree murder. Watching, I just knew it wasn't true because I knew him personally, and I knew he wouldn't hurt anyone. But there it was, saying they were looking for him. I told myself he would be vindicated if they caught him because the innocent didn't get found guilty, and I knew he was innocent. Wondering if I would see him again, I went back to trying to understand my business, all for wanting more for myself, making it all I could concentrate on. This time, I wanted to learn more than I had learned the last time. Who knew it would be this hard to get back in the game? It wasn't easy picking up where I left off, and not once did I think it would be this slow. But with nobody having more patience than me, I just sat back and waited on the money, which didn't come at first, but like I said, I was a patient man. I thought slow money was better than no money.

Also, being realistic, I knew I had to get out and push this stuff if I wanted it to go, which meant I would have to take more risks. And as one of the risks was going to jail, boy, did that keep me in the house more than it let me out. Not one for doing time anymore, especially after being out this long; I like to say I put prison behind me and don't quite think of it as being in front of me. Rolling the dice, I just did me, taking all the punches that were thrown at me. Though life wasn't where I had expected it to be, it wasn't all bad. And what little good did come out of life, I noticed it—so much so because that's how far and in between they were. But I wasn't complaining; I was just determined to get ahead. Once upon a time, I was the man in the world of misfits. Now, I don't know who I am, but I was determined to find out who I was going to be.

Where, on one hand, there was the honest me, and on the other hand, you had the crooked me. Not knowing which way I was going only confused me. No longer having anyone to depend on, I found out I could only depend on myself. Though the world was cruel, I still figured that the good outweighs the bad. I wanted to be a part of this society and not live my life as a convict in the penal society. Knowing that it was better on this side of the fence is the reason I stayed out and got out of a life of crime. But now, I was thinking about getting back in because of my financial situation. I was starving, and nobody would feed me, so I decided to feed myself, even if it meant doing what I didn't want to do. No longer wanting to hurt people only made me wonder if they knew how hunger hurt. With the world being very different now, who's to say life couldn't get better for me?

Finding out if there was a life for me became my goal. How I was going to do that, I didn't know. But hurting, I pressed on, which is what I chose to do instead of lying down and dying. I would go as far as my mental state would let me, loosely not wanting to mess with my brain. But my biggest fear in the world was going crazy and not coming back from it. Already SMI, I tried to stay away from drugs, which usually sent my mind into a world of its own, where the sane me wasn't invited. It was getting harder and harder to stay sane, though fighting with it only made my mind stronger. Learning only to fight on because there was no giving up in me, hoping only to gain where I could afford life because I wanted to live. The only problem was where I wanted to take it - the cops were in my way, looking to stop someone like me at every turn.

Believing that where there's a will, there's a way, I decided to find a path to sell drugs. I scratched and clawed my way into the business. Enlisting the help of my little brother and a few investors, we opened up shop. Initially, things started out well. It only took two or three days to get rid of an ounce, which felt good because it was putting money in my pockets. But it also felt bad because I knew it was wrong. Fighting through the madness didn't stop me from sleeping at night, only because I was eating now. Not having to endure hunger pains made me feel good.

I bought from the little homie who loosely gave me drugs to sell. His working with me helped a lot. Overlooking the shortness of my money only helped me make a little extra, which I needed because I was just getting back in the game. Why that excited me, I don't know, but for the first time in a long time, I was feeling alive. Unable to explain my happiness except for getting back in the game; by now, I had been living in my apartment for a few years. Around this time, my daughter decided to move in, bringing along my granddaughter, who was one of her four girls. Living a good life, she didn't take up much space, making room for the both of them. We coexisted well, which was a good thing. For a moment, I thought I wouldn't have it any other way. But as the saying goes, life goes on, and everybody grows.

At this time, I started feeling guilty about not being able to afford an actual house. Being that I was getting up there in age, I didn't want to leave this earth without leaving them a house. Why was this weighing on me? I didn't know, but all I wanted was to be a good parent, and I didn't know if I was doing that right. Confused, I saw why dreams aren't for people like us. I started wondering, "Are my dreams working for me? Or are they hurting me more for dreaming of them?" Because all I did was try to live up to them, only to see one after another not come true. This is when I started praying for no more dreams as I tried to learn to live without them, calling for reasons to discount them. The only problem was that I could still dream of them. Giving them my all, just to see them fail over and over again, I remembered back to when I had no worries—the last time I called myself living, which was back when I was ten.

I realized I don't call on my dreams because they call on me. Thinking if they call on me, don't they have an obligation to come true? Finding out the hard way that that's not the case, I did everything in my power to work towards the goal of getting them to come true, only to end up wanting to give up, even though I didn't have any give up in me. Not really knowing what I was going through, I watched my mental state take a big hit from my dreams, which made me question them even more. This led me to take these questions to my psychiatrist, whom my clinic had set up for me. They gave me a team to work out my mental state with, trying to bring sanity back into this insane person.

Throughout the years, as I fell in and out of sanity, they never gave up on me, and for the most part, they kept me sane. But they didn't really know how to stabilize me to keep me that way. Though my instability kept me coming back, I felt I needed them. And since it was lifelong, it didn't bother me. I realized I didn't hate the world, but feeling different about people was a whole other story. Knowing what I was capable of doing to them allowed me the certainty that I wouldn't pick up a gun, even though there were situations where I might have. I felt it best to leave them alone. I'm not one to dwell unless there's money involved.

We set up shop in hopes of making enough money to get a spot, and it was working out for the most part. Just as we were about to put a down payment on the spot, something came up that made us have to spend the money on other things, which only kept delaying us from opening up a spot. This caused us to take more penitentiary chances with our curb serving. With a mama as I've got, she didn't raise no fools. Times wouldn't stay the same as peacefully as making a little crack money. I remember sitting at home watching TV when I saw a family member come across the news as someone wanted for first-degree murder. It was something I didn't want to believe. I called one of my little brothers after catching a glimpse of himself on TV. He quickly told me he was in the wind and hung up.

When life goes on, you keep living. Thinking I would never hear from him again, I went about my business as usual, doing the next thing that came to me - trying to figure out how to come up on my next come up. I gave up on the drug game and all. It seemed like I couldn't find anywhere to get it off, so all I was doing was sitting on it. Once I got my last stash off, I just sat at home and tried to save every little dime I could get my hands on, which was hard to do with the bills steadily piling up. But somehow, I managed, only questioning the universe. Not knowing where I belonged made me want to belong.

Finally, some good news came into my family's life—or so everybody thought it was good news. It had to be good news, didn't it? Especially when a close family member hit on the Arizona Scratchers tickets, winning upwards of $500,000. That was supposed to be great news for the family, but like I said, dreams aren't for people like us. Because if we had any hopes of dreaming about that money, we weren't getting any. Upon winning, it went straight to her head. After getting it, she told everybody she would give them some and not to worry, she wouldn't leave them out, which, of course, got everybody's hopes up - until she turned around and busted everybody's bubble, finding excuse after excuse not to give us any money. She turned greedy on everybody, not only leaving us out of the fold but also out of everything that had to do with the money. Taking it every time and keeping it for herself, behind on my bills, I knew she could have helped me out, but she didn't. So, I struggled on.

I continued to make efforts along with everyone else in the family while she lived it up, expecting a little something and getting nothing, which only hurt us. It was harder to live, never expecting family to choose money over us. It only made us want to push on and fight stronger, as we had no choice but to live on.

Life only got harder for us, while for her, it seemed to get easier, spending even up to $300,000. But on what she spent - we didn't know. As life began to get harder for her, she somehow found her way into enjoying the money so much that she ended up having a stroke and was no longer able to enjoy her lavish life. In the long run, she ended up losing her family, with no one wanting to forgive her. So we just took our lives and moved to the other side of town, away from them. All the while, she continued to claim that another family member stole her car and wouldn't give it back. Despite knowing we didn't deserve how she treated us, I still felt like we all continued to love her and that she didn't deserve that stroke. I have a message for her: *"Live your life because I'm going to live mine, with or without you."*

Even though around this time we felt devastated, everybody seemed like they were going through a tough time. Just as a friend of mine went into the mental hospital for about a month and a half to two months. I guess the weight of the world on his shoulders was too much, and he couldn't handle it anymore, so he sought help. This only made me think about my little brother, who everyone thought was losing his mind, too. Only, he was losing it over the drug of his choice. It was taking his brain to places that he couldn't come back from sometimes. Unlike my friend, he wasn't seeking out help, leading him to only smoke more and more of the drug.

This left me to wonder, *is it really real?* And with me fighting my demons, I had to try and clear my own mind. Even though it wasn't the right time, I started to isolate myself from the world, wanting to be left alone. I didn't want to be bothered by anybody. So, I cut off the lights and went into this darkness, dragging out through a bout of depression lasting about six months to a year.

I stayed in that state until my granddaughter and daughter moved in, which brought joy to my life for some time. They made me want to keep going – to not give up on life, which was all I was living for now.

A few months had gone by, and finally, my family member who was on the run gave us a call, letting us know he was safe. He told us that he was ready to still turn himself in, saying he only had to make a little more money to get a lawyer. However, no one in the family was willing to believe him. Even with this, knowing the law wasn't on his side only made him run a little longer. We went without hearing from him for a few more months at a time. As we were worried, we wanted him to come back home, only because we feared he would go down in a shootout with the police, and we didn't want the police to kill him.

Why the family thought he would go out in a blaze of glory, I don't know. But deep down in my heart, I thought he might do it too. From then on, the family tried to talk him into turning himself in every chance they got whenever he called. We were only happy to hear that he was still alive.

That woman from my past - she wanted to come back into my life, and she couldn't see past the world of resentment. She was still fuming from her meanness, and I knew she still wanted to run things. This only reminded me how much I still loved her, but that's the love only I had - lost on her. Though by now, we were friends anyway, so I thought to myself: *why not be her friend and just talk to her?* I mean, I liked it when she talked meanly with me, without knowing that her aggressiveness only turned me on. However, wanting her to see me was the last thing on my mind. Sitting back, I decided to wait to see what would come of that. In my mind, I pledged my loyalty, thinking to myself: *Know this unchanging heart is yours, and I'm ready to show you loyalty from here on out.*

I was hoping that by the time I would be able to get around her defenses, it wouldn't be too late. As time went by, I started to drift further and further apart from her and started to fall more and more for my other girl. So I took it upon myself to let her know lightly. I started off by calling her "baby" every chance I got. One way or another, I was determined to try and win her back, whether she knew it or not. Although she did nothing but look past my every trick, I tried to express my feelings. Every bone in my body kept telling me that I loved her. There was no other way I could explain it. How could I think another way? She was all I thought about and all I dreamt about. I would never have thought otherwise.

Now, this is my promise to you! Knowing dreams aren't for people like us, I'm going to fight this one, coming true with every breath in my body. For you and us, I promise, BABY!

But as the world turns, bringing us to a new day, word has gotten back that my relative, who was on the run for first-degree murder, was no longer on the run. It turns out, he was captured several states away from where he was being charged. He had to go through two months of anxiously waiting to be sent back to face said charges.

Finally, once he was back in his home state, he came to learn that he was up against the death penalty. I never thought it was possible that he could be put to death. Thinking back, I wondered what was going through his mind, so I had a message for him as well. *Are you still dreaming? For you, to have dreamed the dream of ultimate dreams, I understand if you don't dare to dream anymore. Just know, loved one, I love you. I'm ready to listen whenever you need to talk. But as the old saying goes, everybody grows. Nobody knows why we had to part when we parted and went our own ways, still, I continue dreaming the dream of dreams that aren't for people like us.*

www.ingramcontent.com/pod-product-compliance
Lightning Source LLC
Chambersburg PA
CBHW071714140626
46557CB00011B/218

* 9 7 8 1 9 6 4 1 6 5 6 8 4 *